edexcel
advancing learning, changing lives

Preparing to Teach
in the Lifelong Learning Sector

BTEC Level 3

Ben Marshall

Published by
Edexcel Limited
One90 High Holborn
London
WC1V 7BH

www.edexcel.org.uk

Distributed by
Pearson Education Limited
Edinburgh Gate
Harlow
Essex
CM20 2JE

www.longman.co.uk

©Edexcel Limited 2006

First published 2006
10 9 8 7 6 5 4 3 2 1
British Library Cataloguing in Publication Data is available from the
British Library on request

10-digit ISBN 1-84690-024-7
13-digit ISBN 978-1-84690-024-2

Commissioned by Jenni Johns
Cover and text design by Patricia Briggs
Cover image courtesy of PhotoDisc® by Getty ImagesTM
Illustrated by Maria Taylor
Indexed by Martin Hargreaves
Project managed and typeset by Bookcraft Ltd, Stroud, Gloustershire
Printed and bound in Great Britain by Scotprint, Haddington

Acknowledgements
The author wishes to thank Paul Jennings, Izzy Pyle, Sally Martyn and
Jane Boehm for their support and assistance during the writing of this
book.

Page 8 – Mind map by Amy Page and Katie Boehm
Page 19 – Image of gas engineer courtesy of British Gas
Page 39 – Illustration by Patricia Briggs

Page 39 – Bloom's Taxonomy after Bloom, B.S. (1956) *Taxonomy of
Educational Objectives: Handbook 1* New York: Longman
Page 50 – Kolb's Learning Cycle after Kolb, D. (1984) *Experiential
Learning: Experience as the Source of Learning and Development* Upper
Saddle River, NJ: Prentice Hall
Page 62 – Herzberg's motivational factors after Herzberg, F. (1959) *The
Motivation to Work* Hobokem, NJ: John Wiley & Sons Inc.

contents

introduction

This unit, Preparing to Teach, is designed to follow the LLUK Preparing to Teach in the Lifelong Learning Sector. It is designed to meet new national standards in post-16 education and training. The course is suitable for anyone teaching or wishing to teach in colleges, and for those training in industry, business or the public services. This qualification will give you threshold status to teach in the sector. It is the first step towards professional recognition in becoming a teacher, tutor or trainer in the sector.

For the purposes of this book, the generic term 'teacher' refers to teachers, tutors and trainers and 'teach' to teaching, tutoring and training.

When you first look at the book you will discover various icons printed in the margins. These indicate further activities that you can participate in to build and develop your knowledge and understanding. These activities can be found in the book and will enable you to generate evidence for your portfolio.

The icons are:

 Reflection

Reflection marginal notes help you to consider your role and your reaction to themes and ideas presented on the course and in your practice. This is explained in more detail in chapter 1.

 Link to portfolio evidence

These links highlight where the work you produce can be used as evidence towards this qualification. You should store this work in your portfolio of evidence.

Links to assessment objectives show when, where and how work can be used to gain assessment credit.

 Link to assessment objective

Those items with a CD-icon next to them (as below) indicate that further information about the topic can be found on the CD-ROM (which you will find inside the book cover).

You will notice that the CD-ROM has three sections:

1. A section relating directly to the chapters, which gives you interactive quizzes and material to help consolidate what you have just been learning about.

 Link to interactive activity on the CD

2. A section containing guidance relating to building your portfolio, which will help you to understand what evidence and information you will need for your final assessment for this qualification.

Link to portfolio activity on the CD

3. A section containing many different ideas, quotes, hints and suggestions for classroom practice. These have been gathered from experienced teachers who want to give you a helping hand as you take your first steps into teaching.

Link to tool kit activity on CD

The files in the portfolio and toolkits sections have been formatted as Word documents to allow you to customise them to suit your local teaching needs. You may add artwork, photographs, colour, your college logos or anything else that will make them lively and fun to use with your students.

We hope you find the book and CD-ROM helpful on your course, and we wish you the very best for your career in teaching.

Preparing to Teach

step into teaching

Each chapter has a study skills theme running through it. They are signposted in the text and, when the skills may be new, an explanation of the skill is provided. The skill theme for this chapter is 'mind mapping'. Mind mapping is a skill that learners can use to help them creatively, and will be discussed in more detail in this chapter.

study skills
mind
mapping
theme

activity

Who have been the influential teachers in your life? Make notes, and discuss with at least one other person, a list of people who have taught you things throughout your life. Don't be afraid to name names. Tell them who taught you the things that you need to know to do your present job, or to work in the area you would like to teach in.

Teaching and training is something we are all experience from the start. As babies our first teachers were our parents, brothers and sisters. As we grew we got to know many people who filled that role in our life. Some were more influential than others. Some taught us just one thing but that has stayed with us all our lives. This book helps you to take the first steps into becoming a professional teacher, trainer or tutor.

The accompanying CD has quizzes and activities, exercises and resources, which supplement the learning themes of each chapter. It is designed to be interactive and help you through the course. Use the CD to find more detail and to explore areas of special interest. There is a very important section on building your portfolio, please look at this.

The purpose of this book is to introduce you to teaching and training. This book is written to support the Edexcel qualification 'Preparing to Teach'. This is the first step and could lead tp a career in teaching. This book helps you to complete the course. Each chapter refers to the New Professional Standards for Teacher/Tutor/Trainer Education for the Learning and Skills Sector, which are the government's standards for teaching and training in the post-16 sector.

The information in this book is only a start. During the course, you are expected to research your subject, teaching in general and especially the teaching of your subject.

This book is laid out in sections:

Ideas and information are provided to help you through the course.

Activities are designed to give practice with the ideas and relate to the theme of the chapter.

Reflection suggests things that will help you to consider your reactions to ideas and help you to develop as a teacher, trainer or tutor. This should be done on your own. During the course you will be completing a Reflective Practice Journal (RPJ). This is a log or professional development journal. Like a personal diary, it records your thoughts and feelings about issues that occur in teaching, as well as your reactions to issues that arise. The **Reflection** prompts are designed to help you with this. There will be more about the RPJ later in the chapter.

Case studies refer to examples taken from the real world of teaching and training and will help you engage with the text. The names of people and places in these studies have been altered to protect anonymity.

By the end of the book you will have a portfolio of work, which needs to be assessed. At some point you will also need to be assessed in your teaching or training. The comments on the feedback sheets will form part of this collection of evidence and sit in your portfolio.

Evidence
Completing activities that have this icon next to them will provide evidence for your portfolio.

Preparing to Teach

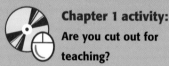

Chapter 1 activity:
Are you cut out for
teaching?

Henrietta came to teaching later in life. She was a professional singer and keyboard player. She had been classically trained.

'I made a good living from touring, I did all sorts, jazz, rock and classical. I sang solo and played in many backing bands. I ended up playing on cruise ships. It sounds glamorous. I travelled the world. But somehow living out of a suitcase was never very much fun, although I have to say the money was tremendous. There was little security. There was no way of saying what would happen after the tour or the cruise was over. I did love performing most of the time but it had its downsides as well. Working in the pit at a West End theatre every night in the dead of winter was perhaps the low point.

I had no qualifications, but with the money I saved I put myself through Bath University. Because I had always enjoyed helping younger performers in the band, I then did teaching qualifications. All the way through I supported myself and when I finally taught it was to adults in London. It's great to be able to pass on my knowledge and skills. I find them highly motivated and I never regretted making this move, albeit later in life.'

Why did Henrietta become a teacher? What regrets might she have as a result?

Your RPJ, or log, is something you should use all the time in the course. How you set it out is up to you; a suggested format is given on the CD. You will have to show your RPJ to your tutor for this course, but that is all: it will be private. It gives you an opportunity to record things as they occur and a great chance to look back on how things are going. Reflection is good. It is an essential part of getting to know something and in getting to know ourselves. It is useful to keep personal diaries. The RPJ is the same sort of thing, but relates to this course. Reflection in teaching helps us not only to assess our development, but it can help us to identify our strengths and highlight areas where we can develop.

'Nothing is more dangerous than an idea, when you only have one idea.' – Alain

Mind maps are a different way of taking notes, generating ideas, solving issues and helping create solutions. Originating centuries ago, but recently made popular by Tony Buzan, mind maps abandon the list of standard note taking. Instead they use a sketch lay out. A mind map shows the 'shape' of something, the worth of different items and the way in which one item relates to another.

By using mind maps, you can quickly understand something and the way facts fit together. Mind maps support creative thinking in a way you will find easy to remember.

Mind maps are a great place to start planning something such as an essay or an assignment. They help you to organise ideas. Put the focus in the centre or your map and think about all the alternative ideas, and how they link together. They are also a useful way of taking notes in a lecture.

Reflection

What first made you want to teach? Was it the money? Was it the security? Are you a caring person who has a genuine need to help? Is it because of the impression left by your experiences in teaching? Is it a combination of these or another reason? Write it down, then put the sheet at the front of your PDJ. It will be interesting to look at it later on.
What do you want out of the course? What do you expect to get out of it?

activity

What makes a good teacher? Use a mind map to organise your ideas and write a short statement (not more than 200 words) on what you believe are the qualities of a good teacher.

activity

During this course you will see teachers and trainers lead sessions. These should be primarily in your own subject. If you want to watch other areas as well that is fine and can be very useful. Make a list of teachers or trainers you would like to see including a one or two line explanation of why. Discuss this with at least one other person.

activity

Preparing to Teach

Draw your own mind map that centres on teaching or training. Explain the reasons why you are interested in teaching as a career, and how you came into teaching. Consider what it is that makes you believe you will be able to teach, how great a commitment it will be to do this course and how you see yourself in 10 year's time. Using the mind map as a basis, discuss teaching and what it means to you with at least one other person.

When making your own mind maps remember that they are for your own use and need not make sense to anyone else. Using colour and pictures are great to really help you remember things.

To make a mind map:

- Write the title of the subject in the centre of the page and draw a circle around it. This is shown by the circle in the example.

- For the major headings, draw lines out from this circle and label them.

- If you have another level of information belonging to the headings, draw these and link them to the heading lines.

- For individual facts or ideas, draw lines out from the heading lines and label them.

- As you come across new facts, link them in to your mind map.

Mind maps are a powerful tool but mind maps are not:

- Intended for anyone else to use

- A solution on their own, and should not be submitted as completed work

- Totally new, they are just a different way of helping you to think.

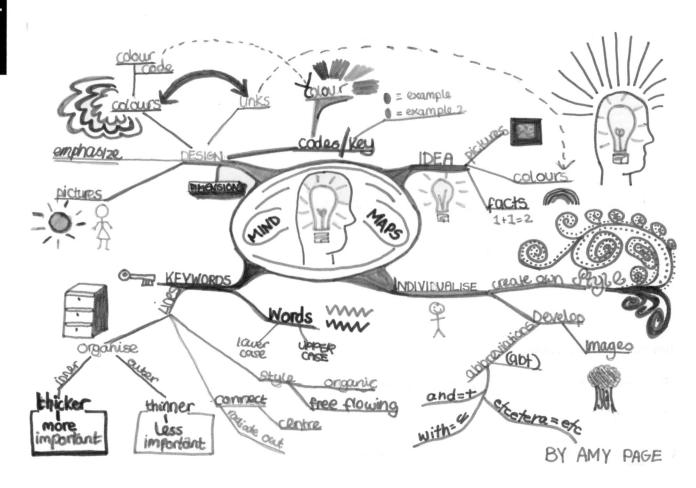

BY AMY PAGE

Bryn, a qualified electrician, learnt his trade through apprenticeship and a full-time course at the local college. He says that he learnt most of the theories and procedures at college. Bryn learnt through formal lectures and workshop sessions. The apprenticeship was practising the things he learnt at college. He found that actually doing something was his best way of learning.

'My best lecturer was Mr Lawrence because he made the theories come alive and gave real examples. He would explain in such a way that anyone could understand. He was open and very approachable, always patient. I learnt a lot from him, as did all the students. He had a great enthusiasm for the subject and was always up to date, something you have to be if you are in this trade. He always related things to the real world. He had been a tradesman and I think we all could relate to that.'

Teachers are all around us and certain dedicated individuals see this as a career. We are not all equipped to teach, and some of us would not want to even try.

A good teacher needs to be many things. They must be organised and able to keep time excellently, they need compassion, dedication, a genuine love of and a thorough knowledge of their subject. Teachers need these qualities and they must also be: an effective communicator; responsive; innovative; creative; and inclusive in their approach.

It is a long list and most teachers do not have all of these qualities when they start, but develop them through doing the job. However, there is one essential quality without which teachers really find it hard to do their job: that quality is enthusiasm.

What then do teachers need to be aware of?

They need to know about:

- Learners and their individual barriers to communication

- When learners are lacking in motivation

- The dangers of making assumptions about learners

Preparing to Teach

- Caring too little or too much, which impedes learning

- Knowing when to say no

- Knowing and understanding the issues of a challenging learner

- Managing learning rather than controlling learners.

However, teaching is not:

- A cushy number

- A good way of making money; there are many different sorts of people on the *Sunday Times* rich list and none of them are teachers

- A part-time job; if the hours are part-time the commitment is not

- A job to do while the children are at school.

It is no wonder that good teachers are well regarded by society and so in demand. Teachers do not earn a fortune, but it is an honest wage. Teaching is fulfilling and it is satisfying – helping your fellow human beings.

If you feel for the human race and you want it to survive. If you feel for the next generation and you want it to be better equipped to face the challenges of this century. If you want to share your know-how. If you want the human race to develop and want it to succeed. If you care. If you have an irresistible impression left by an educational experience. If you are creative and want an outlet for those things that drive you. Then teaching and training is the career for you and this book will help you to get there.

summary

In this chapter we learnt about the development of teaching and learning. We have examined your first experiences of teaching and learning. The purpose and the layout of this book has been discussed, along with the professional development journal or PDJ, mind maps and their uses. We have identified the qualities a teacher has, what learners expect from teachers, what teachers need to be aware of with respect to learners and the teaching profession, and its limitations.

resources

Buzan, T. and Buzan, B. (2006) *The Mind Map Book* Harlow: Pearson.

Preparing to Teach

In this chapter, I have learnt about:

- [ ] This book and how to use it
- [ ] The development of teaching and learning
- [ ] My early experiences of teaching
- [ ] Mind maps
- [ ] Reflective Practice Journal
- [ ] The qualities of a teacher
- [ ] Learners and their expectations
- [ ] Teaching as a job

your role and your responsibilities

subject

Your role and responsibilities.

learning outcomes

In chapter you will learn how to:

- Explain your own role, responsibilities and the boundaries of your role as a teacher or trainer.
  Assessment criteria 1.1

- Explain key aspects of current legislative requirements and the codes of practice within a specific context.
  Assessment criteria 1.2

- Identify the potential learning needs of learners and the potential points of referral.
  Assessment criteria 1.3

- Identify issues of equality and diversity, and ways to promote inclusion.
  Assessment criteria 1.4

- Explain the need for record keeping.
  Assessment criteria 1.5

- Understand your own role, responsibilities and the boundaries of your role as a teacher or trainer.
  Assessment criteria 1.6

study skills **research** *theme*

Case study

Toni is a lecturer in English at a FE college. We asked her to list all the things she felt she had to do when she was in charge of a group of learners. This is the list she came up with:

- Do the administration – includng registers and other records
- Assess ongoing individual skills
- Assess ongoing individual abilities in the subject for which I teach
- Assess the learners at the end of the course – mark the exams
- Timekeeping
- Be an information technology wizard
- Keep up to date with my subject
- Keep up to date with my professional qualifications
- Attend meetings
- Be observed by the college management and the Ofsted inspectors
- Action emails
- Talk to learners on a one-to-one casual basis outside the classroom
- Plan courses
- Plan visits to industrial locations
- Teach.

activity

How does this list compare to yours? Draw a mind map, or write notes, to discuss with at least one other person the duties of a teacher.

chapter 2 **your role and your responsibilities**

We have discovered that teachers and trainers are all around us and have been so since the beginning of time. We have also identified that the best teachers and trainers are special people who are experts in their own field and have the know-how to pass these skills and specialised knowledge onto learners.

activity

Use mind mapping to describe what you would expect to do in your dream job as a teacher.

Teachers have a great many things they have to do. Perhaps the most important is passing on what they know about a certain area or subject and ensuring that learners have enough practice and motivation to pass the course. We trust teachers to do this. Trust is at the centre of the teacher or trainer's role. Learners trust the person in front of them to provide them with the skills and knowledge at the start of their career.

activity

What do learners expect from the teacher who is leading the group? Write a list of as many expectations as you can think of and discuss it with someone else in the group.

Study skills

Research is a quest and can be exciting, informative and educational. However, we often jump into research and get lost because we haven't thought things through. A little planning at the start can be very beneficial. Research is not a linear process. You should try to use as many sources as possible at the beginning to get as wide a picture as you can.

Sit down for a few minutes and think about what you already know about the subject, what you need to find out and how you are going to use your findings.

Then draw a mind map, sketch out ideas or write notes to help you when you start the process. Think how you are going to discover the information – read? interview experts? watch videos? visit libraries or museums? observe people in action? use the Internet? From this some key words should emerge. Use these ideas to help your search.

activity

Use research skills to find an example of an actual job description for teaching. You may need to be diplomatic if you are asking teachers who are in post.

Harvard referencing

Then start your quest, use the Internet and libraries to find books and other information. Start reading, watching videos, interviewing experts, asking colleagues, listening to tapes or the radio, observing people in action or whatever is apt. You don't need to read the books from cover to cover, or listen to the whole tape or watch all the video; just find the information relevant to your search. (Don't forget to record the details of books and other sources you use. It is essential you give these as a list of references at the end of articles that you write. You must provide information about the book title, the author and the year of publication. You need to give credit for the ideas and not claim them for yourself.)

Take notes as you go and when you have finished use these as the basis for the finished work. As stated before, don't worry if topics for research occur to you while you are writing. When this happens you can do some extra research. However, don't lose sight of the end product and let the research get in the way of deadlines.

Here are some advertisements taken from a trade journal for teaching posts.

Lecturer in Numeracy

To collaborate in the implementation of the Numeracy strand of the Continuing Professional Development programme.
To contribute to the development, delivery and evaluation of adult Numeracy-related teacher training, projects, and other work of the LLLU.
To work with the specialist Numeracy team to develop the services to be provided by the new Numeracy professional development centre.
To develop study packs and online learning resources for adult Numeracy teachers and teacher trainers.
To undertake other duties when and as required by the director of the Unit.

Lecturer
(Electrical Installation)

The role will include teaching, learners reviews, tutorial, and some course development. You will be self motivated, and well organised as you will spend your time teaching and preparing lessons for people who are involved with this area of industry. You will have good personal and organisational skills that enable you to communicate effectively with other team members, learners, apprentices and their employers.

Lecturer in Beauty Therapy

A highly motivated person is required to teach and assess a range of Beauty Therapy programmes. You must have a recognised professional qualification together with recent industrial experience.

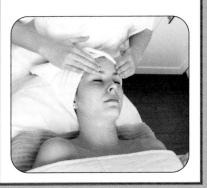

Reflection
How does this compare with what you feel a teacher should be asked to do? In what ways do you feel you will be making a compromise between what you want to do (your dream job) and the reality of the job descriptions in the case study?

Preparing to Teach

activity

We should be aware of the government expectations and requirements for teaching and training. Research what these standards are – the websites the government has set up should assist here. When you have finished researching draw a mind map titled 'New Standards for Teachers and Trainers' then write a 500 word (about one-page) report on your findings.

New standards

Explain key aspects of current legislative requirements and the codes of practice.

It is obvious in some fields that we need to keep on top of current legislation, for example a police officer can't do their job properly without being aware of all the changes in the legal system, and how this effects their role. For example, changes in the speed limit are something that they need to know about. Without that knowledge they can't do their job properly. Within teaching there are similar legislative changes that you, as a professional, need to keep on top of. One change that happened in the last few years refers to reforms to initial teacher training for the learning and skills sector; something that affects all of us within the sector. There are too many changes to list in such a short publication. Some examples, however, are changes in:

◣ the Sector Skill Council – Lifelong Learning UK

◣ the National Training Organisations – ENTO

◣ the Awarding Bodies – Edexcel.

These are all things we need to be aware of. It is our job as professionals to keep up to speed with this. In universities it is thought so essential that lecturers are paid to attend conferences and write papers that discuss current issues. The human resources manager or the professional development manager should help to keep staff up to date in any organisation.

New standards

activity

Research and make a list of all the sources you can think of that would enable you to keep up to date with your subject, and with teaching in general. Produce evidence to show that you have accessed at least five of these in the last month.

case studies

Jasmine qualified as a heating engineer in 1991 from a Yorkshire Technical College. She has been working as a self-employed plumber for the last 15 years, specialising in the installation and maintenance of central heating systems, usually for clients she has built up over the years. Recently, she has had a number of contracts withdrawn as the developers said she does not have Corgi status. At first she thought it was a joke, but now has come to understand the seriousness of the situation; and that she has fallen behind with her qualifications. She feels it is partly due to her being self-employed, working in isolation and not keeping up to date with the changes in the laws. She now feels that it may be too late for her to get the status necessary for her to carry on in her job.

Preparing to Teach

After a sticky period, Jasmine was offered a job with British Gas who put her through her Corgi registration and now pay her to keep up to date. She finds this job rewarding and far more secure.

Was Jasmine able to keep up to date? What was her favourite way of keeping up to date? What were the consequences for her of not doing this? What is your method of keeping up to date? What are the issues at present in your industry?

We can research changes in current legislation and how it affects us in a variety of ways. The Internet is a great way to access this information 24 hours a day.

Brian runs a successful and happy department within a college in inner London. We asked the staff why this department was so happy and what made it tick. Many pointed out the good professional working atmosphere, that Brian is always able to support them. They feel he is approachable and honest, trustworthy and diligent, but more than anything most pointed to how he is continuously updating them on things that affect their jobs. Such activity might be: news of inspections and Ofsted's expectations; jobs and new opportunities; the latest government initiatives or to do with individual learners. In all ways, they feel they are doing a good job and are happy. They don't ever feel exposed and are keen to talk to each other about current changes that affect them. The staff turnover is low.

What things did Brian do to keep his staff up to date? What methods did Brian use? What were the consequences of Brian doing it? How does this compare to your present workplace?

Health and safety

RPJ – swot analysis

Reflection

How does all this change make you feel? Is it good to be part of an ever-changing and developing profession that adapts to meet the needs of individuals and society in general? Are you pleased that the government is interested in education and training and sees it as one of the most important things in shaping the future world? Are you concerned about the job you are getting into? Is it more than you had bargained for?

Evidence

Complete this activity and keep a record in your portfolio

It is your duty to be aware of the latest health and safety legislation and how that affects your job. In some industries health and safety is all important; in others its importance is more subtle. Being in charge of a group of learners has its own health and safety implications. For example, it is your duty to make sure that all individuals are aware of fire exits and means of evacuation. It is also essential that individuals know where the nearest toilets are.

activity

Research health and safety legislation. Write a short account (500 words) of what changes you can see being necessary and how current health and safety legislation affects teaching in your area. Use a particular group of learners to illustrate your points.

Preparing to Teach

Identify the potential learning needs of learners and the potential points of referral for the learners.

We need to understand the way people learn so that we can pass on knowledge and skills in a suitable way for everyone. We must also know what learners expect to get from this training or teaching. We should be aware of any special requirements that learners have, and anything essential that stands in the way of learning for which we may need special support.

We all understand information in different ways. According to current research, these ways of learning, or learning styles as they have come to be known, can be divided into three main types (illustrated right and below):

- visual (through the eyes – seeing and reading)

- auditory (through the ears – listening)

- kinaesthetic (learning by doing – touching and doing).

In some types of learning, information gained through the other senses (for example, smell and taste in cooking) can be equally important and all can come together as multi-sensory learning.

Visual auditory kinaesthetic (VAK) learning styles

According to the VAK model, most people have a favoured learning style, although, in practice, we usually use a mixture of all three. We can find out which is favoured by each individual by a simple testing based on people's history and experiences. We can present things to suit people's preferred learning styles, but usually with a group a combination of all three styles works well.

Visual
The use of pictures, diagrams, demonstrations, handouts, films and so on.

Auditory
Transferring skills and knowledge through listening to an instructional lecture, for example.

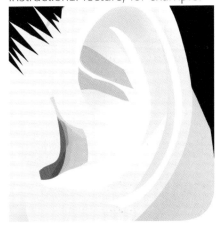

Kinaesthetic
Learning by doing – touching, feeling, holding, practical hands-on experiences.

Preparing to Teach

We all learn through using different senses and combinations of these senses. Each of us has a preferred learning style, which usually is a combination of all three.

Reflection

How did you find information easiest to absorb throughout your formal and informal education? Now you understand your preferred learning style, how might you improve the notes you write and the way you learn?

Evidence

Complete this activity and keep a record in your portfolio

activity

Research VAK learning styles. Draw a mind map of your preferred learning styles, identified by your research, and then test it on the CD.

Using the mind map as a reference, present a two- or three-minute talk on your preferred learning style.

Use visual aids, and any other sort of aids, to help you explain your preferred learning style, and that of your parents (or two other people you know very well). Find out from your audience what they thought of your presentation, and what they understood your preferred learning style to be.

case study

Phil learnt his trade as a mechanic partly through formal classes at the local college and partly through training on the job. He found that practical sessions were both more fun and more instructive. He says he learnt far more actually doing the job. The theories were something he had to do, but it was difficult and he didn't enjoy the lessons; often getting in to trouble.

How does Phil absorb information? If he was in your group, how would you present a new piece of legislation regarding central heating boilers to him?

Preparing to Teach

case study

Andrea is taking a refresher course in reflexology at a central London College. She finds the lectures both enlightening and interesting; she finds the practical sessions a little tedious and can't wait to put her newly acquired theories into practice.

Identify what Andrea's preferred learning style is and explain how you would make the classes more interesting for her. Discuss, or write notes, to record your views.

activity

Are all learning styles equally important? Are they all equally important to the learners you have had experience of? Consider some learners you know. Rank each learning style in order of importance and its implication for learning.

Exploration of equality and diversity and ways to promote inclusion.

It is not just our conscience that tells us to offer equal opportunities to all our learners; it is enshrined in law. There are many laws which support our stance that we should not be prejudiced against learners on grounds of gender, sexual orientation, race, religion, colour, age or whether or not they have a learning difficulty, a disability or any other characteristics. Learners and staff alike should feel valued and have a fair and equitable quality of working life and learning experience whatever their characterisitcs. We should aim to promote equality and diversity, and value the benefits it brings. Of course we should be properly briefed before learners join us.

activity

Find out what is meant by equality at work and in education. Find at least three examples of this and be prepared to present a two- to three-minute talk on this to a colleague. Discuss your findings and come up with as many real examples as you can of how you would use equality in your work as a teacher.

Lesson planning

Preparing to Teach

If there is no selection and assessment prior to the group starting, it is up to us to discover the individuals' diverse abilities and to use this in our delivery with the group.

Increasing numbers of schools are finding they are unable to address some of the more basic needs of learners. This becomes particularly apparent when preparing learners for the end-point of their secondary education and the GCSE examinations. Following the introduction of league tables based on achievement, the presence of learners who are less academically inclined increasingly becomes an issue as teachers focus on activities in the classroom that are linked to examinations.

Every school has students whose needs are not being met by the more traditional approaches to teaching and learning adopted to suit the majority. Schools may lack the time or resources to address the specific needs of a small proportion of their learners who are neither interested nor involved in the range of subjects on offer in the curriculum. The result is that these learners may well become disinterested at best and disaffected or disruptive at worse. To address the needs of some learners, and to have something as an alternative to the more academic subjects, Increased Flexibility Programmes (IFP) have been developed in further education. Often these strategies come too little and too late. Young people may have already been excluded from full-time education. These students are the target for inclusion projects created by some centres.

 **Group contract**

Preparing to Teach

activity

What do you feel are the likely consequences of excluding so many children from school? – For society? For the children? Discuss this topic with at least one other person and write up a set of notes, or a mind map, showing your views.

case study

The New Day Project

The **New Day Project Group** are young people who have been excluded because of disruptive behaviour, bullying, inappropriate language or behaviour, violence against staff and other pupils, drink or drug-related issues, prostitution, mental problems, self-harming and any other category of problems that the referring schools feel unable to manage. From the learners' perspective, they feel they have been failed by a school system that caters for those with academic goals, but offers few alternatives. Another complaint frequently made by the young people themselves is that school was 'boring'. For 'boring' read 'failing to interest'. For 'failing to interest' read failing to recognise or appreciate individual needs. This in part reflects the training, or lack of staff training in dealing with this increasingly volatile section of the school population. It also reflects the pressures placed on schools to ensure learners perform to the accepted norms. The school system fails to be inclusive because of lack of resources or expertise and, therefore, is unable to deliver equality of opportunity or diversity within the curriculum.

activity

What does the term inclusive mean in this case? How did the young people feel about education in general and their schools in particular?

The individuals

Sarah is 15 years of age. She is bright, attractive and wants to learn. Her mother is a working prostitute and is never around during the evenings to ensure that Sarah does her homework. Neither can she supervise what Sarah gets up to when she is not there. Therefore, Sarah goes out every night, and is a member of a gang that spends its evening drinking vodka in a local park. Sarah's ability to concentrate is extremely limited. She is prone to sudden, violent outbursts – largely a result of her frustration at not being able to get on with her school work. She was permanently excluded from school as the staff could not control her behaviour.

Shane is 14 years old. He is slow, sullen and hides under his 'hoody'. He avoids any form of communication. Shane's mother is loud and aggressive. His father is unemployed and, after a drink or two can be handy with his belt, fist or anything else that comes to hand. Shane's father is always quick to blame, especially Shane. In school, Shane has become totally uncooperative. He drives the class teacher to distraction and it has come to the point where there is little reason to keep Shane in the classroom.

Ben is 15 years of age. He is highly excitable. He has Attention Deficit Hyperactivity Syndrome (ADHD) and is unable to settle for any length of time, or to focus on work. Ben's parents are supportive, but have a limited effect on his behaviour as there is little real communication within the family. Ben has been permanently excluded from school due to his inappropriate behaviour in the classroom. His language and behaviour made the female teacher feel intimated, although no actual threat was made.

Bryony is 15 years old. She is relatively bright and very sociable, but easily led. She is very aware of her peer group and, although she wants to do well at school, it is not seen to be cool so she is disruptive in class. She lacked concentration and exhibited challenging behaviour. Eventually, Bryony was excluded as a disruptive element.

activity

How does the experience of these students represent a lack of equal opportunities? Are there any ways you can think of to give these students a fresh start?

The outcome – an inclusive approach

These four learners came together as a part of the inclusion project in a college of further education, as part of a special 'unit'. They were provided with their own area and administrative set-up, with specialist staff and a high staff-to-learner ratio and the help of special support staff. The teaching was based on Individual Learning Plans (ILPs) in which each learner was provided with the opportunity to identify where their weaknesses were, and what they felt were the strategies that would best help them achieve. Each morning, learners would arrive in their area and were given the opportunity to socialise over their 'breakfast club' – making tea, coffee and toast for themselves, and each other, with the equipment that was provided for them. In this way, all learners had their basic needs for food, drink and warmth met before the start of the 'working day'. Sessions formed a broad curriculum – with mathematics, English, art and design forming the core. Within sessions, each learner is supported – usually on a one-to-one basis – around their negotiated personal goals. Where concentration spans are short, learners are rewarded with breaks. When behaviour becomes erratic, they have the opportunity for a 'time-out' – when they leave the room to calm down. They then have the responsibility for returning and carrying on with their work when they are ready. Because they are given control rather than being controlled, it provides them with the opportunity for developing social skills and self-management skills. Where there are serious anger-management issues, they are provided with additional, specialist support as appropriate.

Equal opportunities is a policy taken seriously by all providers of education and training at all levels. It is the basis of much good work. The New Day Project was a special case where individual programmes were designed and the outcome was excellent. The participants are all well on their way to rejoining mainstream schooling.

activity

What are the issues of equality and diversity within the New Day Project? Give examples of issues and how they were resolved.

activity

What other issues does equal opportunities cover? Research and list the range of issues you feel could be considered in this area.

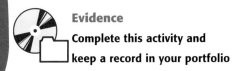

Evidence
Complete this activity and keep a record in your portfolio

case study

Sarah was diagnosed with a neurological disease when she was eight. It has meant that she is confined to a wheelchair for most of the day and evening. She now lives on her own, within a small south-west London community. She found it difficult to get anywhere in formal education at school. Now in her early 20s, she feels that she has the potential to study at a higher level. After initial discussions with a deputy head of department at a local college, and two one-hour tests, it was felt it would be best for her to take an Access course. This is a course that prepares people with little or no formal qualifications for a degree. With the assistance of the college staff, she was able to take her place on the course.

activity

What issues would you imagine Sarah faced returning to formal education after so long? What issues did the staff that instructed her have to overcome when preparing lessons? What extra help would a learner like Sarah receive in your organisation? Obtain copies of the equal opportunities policy from your organisation.

Evidence
Complete this activity and keep a record in your portfolio

New standards

We must consider equal opportunities when addressing all groups of learners, this may require extra preparation. It is always time well spent. Meeting the diverse needs of individual learners is a challenge that provides the cornerstone of successful teaching and learning.

activity

Write a short essay (500 words) on why it is important to address the issues of equality, diversity and inclusion within your teaching or training area.

Evidence
Complete this activity and keep a record in your portfolio

Explain the need for record keeping.   Assessment criteria 1.5

We base so much of what we do as teachers on the records we keep of individual learners. Records can be informative, help us to build a picture of our learners and help us to design courses to suit them. There is almost always a course outcome that is recorded for information purposes and for evidence towards a final qualification. Keep in mind what records you are keeping, for whom and why. Records are kept in many ways but the most common way today is on a computer, often using a spreadsheet.

Many organisations use a standard form for keeping records; this is usually the case with class registers and student grades. Your organisation can also provide guidance on keeping progress records.

Within formal education, record-keeping is used to assist decision-making. The evidence we collect can inform those trying to make decisions about whether courses should be run. Our records assist the inspectors and the quality assurance divisions of a college. Records are also very informative for the individual teacher; they can provide feedback about our performance. Many teachers and trainers find it useful to keep an accurate personal diary, and to compare this to the records.

Reflection

How do you feel about record keeping and paperwork in general? Make notes on your feelings.

case study

Bernard teaches dance in an HE college.

'I'm a full-time dance teacher, teaching in groups, and I see over 100 students each week – I haven't got time to plan or keep records, anyway in my area what's the point? The students can either dance or not at the end of the course. And I can assure you mine can dance! I think the Royal Ballet would agree with me.'

Would you sympathise with this statement? Make notes of your response, and the suggested way you could talk to Bernard.

In this chapter we learnt about job descriptions, about your role, the expectations of different groups and individuals, how we can understand more about learners and when it may be best to ask for specialised help. We saw how a teacher needs to keep updating their knowledge about legislation and government directives. Teachers also need to keep up to date with professional development and changes in their area of work. We came to an understanding of how teaching identifies and supports issues of equality in opportunity. We also saw how we embrace diversity and encourage inclusion. We used research as a study skill throughout. We discovered the importance of keeping accurate and up-to-date records.

Resources

The BBC

The Teaching Channel on satellite television

Some useful websites are:

www.new-oceans.co.uk
www.lifelonglearninguk.org
www.successforall.gov.uk
www.dfes.gov.uk
www.trainingmatters.org.uk
www.trainingfoundation.com
www.ofsted.gov.uk
www.tes.co.uk.

Some other sources are:

Trade Publications in your area of work

Organisation news publications

Formal and informal meetings with colleagues

Meetings with external verifiers and moderating authorities

Local libraries – the reference section usually carries a good stock of journals.

Preparing to Teach

In this chapter, I have learnt about:

- ☐ Job descriptions
- ☐ Responsibilities and roles
- ☐ Identifying learner needs
- ☐ Keeping up to date and informed
- ☐ Ensuring equality of opportunity

- ☐ Ensuring inclusion
- ☐ Ensuring health and safety considerations are included in all sessions
- ☐ Research
- ☐ Record keeping

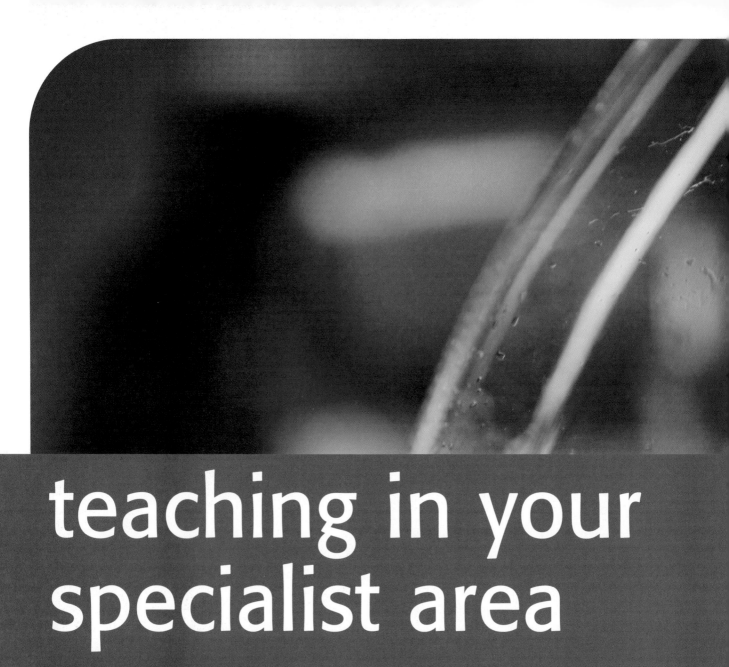

teaching in your specialist area

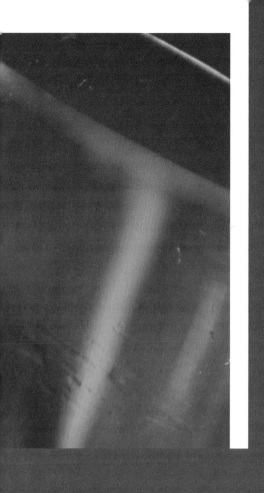

chapter 3

subject

Understand and demonstrate appropriate teaching and learning approaches in the specialist area.

learning outcomes

In this chapter you will learn how to:

- Identify and demonstrate relevant approaches to teaching and learning in relation to the specialist area.

  Assessment criteria 2.1

- Explain ways to embed elements of functional skills in the specialist area.

  Assessment criteria 2.2

- Justify selection of teaching and learning approaches for a specific session.

  Assessment criteria 2.3

study skills
theme

keeping
up to date

Identify and demonstrate relevant approaches to teaching and learning in relation to the specialist area. Assessment criteria 2.1

It is important that you identify the area in which you plan to teach. You might choose this area based on the subject you studied at university or college. You might choose based on your work experience, or because you have particular interest in an area, or you may have been working in an area for some years and built expertise in your field.

Once you have made your choice, you should talk to an experienced teacher and ask them if you can observe them delivering a session.

We can learn so much by observing experienced people doing their job. This is the underlying theory of apprenticeships: experienced people show you how to do the job and supervise you through all the learning stages (as defined by Bloom – see page 39). Observing skilled teachers and trainers at work in our specialist area can help to confirm whether this is really the job that we want to do.

activity

Imagine you have arranged to observe an experienced teacher deliver a session in your specialist area. (An experienced teacher is usually considered to be someone who is fully qualified and has more been working in the area for three years.)

Draw a mind map of the things that you will want to observe, and the questions that you would want to ask.

Design a checklist that you could use for this observation. What other things might you need to do or think about before you go in to this session?

Preparing to Teach

chapter 3 **teaching in your specialist area**

Teachers or trainers are keen to introduce new people to their subject area. However, please remember they will not be paid for this intrusion, so it is polite to give them notice and to let them know what you will be observing. It is not your job to participate in the lesson, just to observe.

When you start teaching, your sessions will be observed by a senior teacher or trainer. Most organisations have standard forms for lesson or session observation, with a section for feedback. Feedback can provide a positive basis for improvement of practice and future professional development.

The Office for Standards in Education (Ofsted) is responsible in England for setting and monitoring standards in education. Teachers and trainers may also be observed by Ofsted inspectors when delivering a session. Ofsted has its own form for recording lesson observations.

Reflection
Use a mind map to record your thoughts and then produce a list. How would you like to be observed? Which session would you most like to be observed delivering?

activity

Draw a mind map to form the basis for a discussion, with at least one other person, on the subject of observing lessons. What are your feelings about an observation form? Would you be happy to be assessed in this way? Find out what the procedure is for observing the session of an individual teacher in your institution or organisation.

activity

Research a recent scheme of work or training proposal for your area of speciality. Discuss its strengths with at least one other person.

The development of skills is specific to our teaching or training area. In cooking, we try to develop the students' sense of taste. Many teachers or trainers in this area find comparison and blind-tasting to be useful techniques to strengthen ideas and skills. This skill is really not important when studying mathematics, for example. In other areas different skills are important. Touch is vital when training someone in individual instrumental skills in music. Developing the sense of smell is a useful skill when training wine tasters.

Preparing to Teach

Learning styles

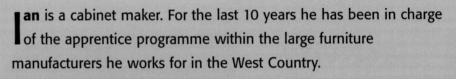
case studies

Ian is a cabinet maker. For the last 10 years he has been in charge of the apprentice programme within the large furniture manufacturers he works for in the West Country.

> 'One of the things that I find I have to train people in is developing their sense of touch. It is essential in my field. An educated finger tip can tell you when a piece of joinery is satisfactory. It is the only way to do it. I have tried measurement but even the finest measuring device does not compare with an educated touch.'

What learning styles are used by Ian? How can you use them in your teaching or training?

Bernice teaches on many courses about wine appreciation and vintner studies in general.

> 'A good balance between current information, and an understanding of science are important. A student won't get very far without researching this old and interesting area, but the most important thing is developing a sense of taste. "Mouth feel" is another thing that is very important with wines.'

What are the things we can learn about from these two statements?

Explain ways to embed elements of functional skills in the specialist area.

Assessment criteria 2.2

Skills are the ability to so something well, especially something manual or physical. We are born with certain skills such as the ability to breathe, but we also acquire skills throughout our life with the help of others; for example, learning to walk and talk. There are some skills that we all need to learn to function properly and be able to do a job of work. We all need basic skills in communication and so need to learn to speak, read and write. We also all need some level of basic skill when using numbers. Teachers and trainers can demonstrate the importance of basic skills by showing how they can be used within their specialised area, and by giving their learners plenty of practice in using these skills.

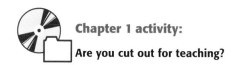

Chapter 1 activity:
Are you cut out for teaching?

case study

Preparing to Teach

Beatrice trains mechanics for a major motor manufacturer. She gives regular up-dating sessions for new products.

'Increasingly I find that the engineers these days need to be able to use computerised equipment. We have microchips inside the engines of our cars, which are constantly adjusting all sorts of things within the engine. A computer connected to the engine of the car can give us all sorts of information. It is in the interest of individual service stations to use this information to keep the cars running at optimum performance. New recruits who come to us and are not computer literate find it difficult at first. Most soon develop the skills however when they see the need to use the equipment and how much better their job becomes as a result.'

Beatrice's background is not in mechanics.

'I have been a trainer in IT since the nineties. I have always been interested in motors, my father was a mechanic and ran his own small service station. When I was approached to take charge of the training I saw this as a chance to get back into an area I loved and to use the skills I had developed over the years as well.'

What skills are important when training as a mechanic these days? Beatrice's background training is not in mechanics, how does her training equip her to do her present job? What skills does she bring to the job?'

We all need to be aware of the use of skills in our work. In recent years, information communication technology (ICT) skills have developed rapidly and these days it is unusual to do any job where they are not involved.

activity

With reference to the experienced teacher you previously observed in your specialist area, how did they incorporate skills in their teaching? Was there anything more that they could have done? How did that teacher keep up to date in their subject? How would you incorporate the basic skills of communication and numeracy into your sessions?

Learner tasks

Skills are so important that we should make every effort to incorporate and flag them in all our learner tasks. It helps to identify where you are for the learners. They want to know that you are linking to other areas and reinforcing skills.

So far we have been thinking about teaching as a general skill. This is true to a large extent, however there are types of teaching that are different, and areas that require special skills and even different learning styles.

Chapter 2 activity:

What is your learning style?

Chapter 3 activity:

Getting the method right

Reflection

Which ideas regarding teaching do you think are good and useful? How will you use them in your teaching?

Evidence

Complete this activity and keep a record in your portfolio

activity

Produce a learner task for a course that you deliver, or one where you would like to teach, that clearly shows how the skills of communication, number and ICT might be involved.

Preparing to Teach

Justify selection of teaching and learning approaches for a specific session.

Assessment criteria 2.3

We tend to learn things when we need to. According to Bruner (1960), 'interest in the material to be learned is the best stimulus to learning'. Once learners are on our programmes (and we believe it is because they need the knowledge, skills and understanding we offer) how do they acquire information and skills? An understanding of this process leads to better training and teaching sessions. In 1956, B.S. Bloom developed his theory about the way we learn. Much of it is still applicable today. Bloom disagreed that education was about mere fact transfer; it is about mastery. When learners have mastered a skill or some knowledge, then we can consider our job done. Learners acquire information in three different ways: they want knowledge, skills and to understand what they are doing.

The stages of truly mastering something are:

- when learners recognise it

- when learners can show they understand it

- when learners are able to apply their skill or knowledge to a real-life situation

- when learners are able to use the new information to analyse a real-life situation.

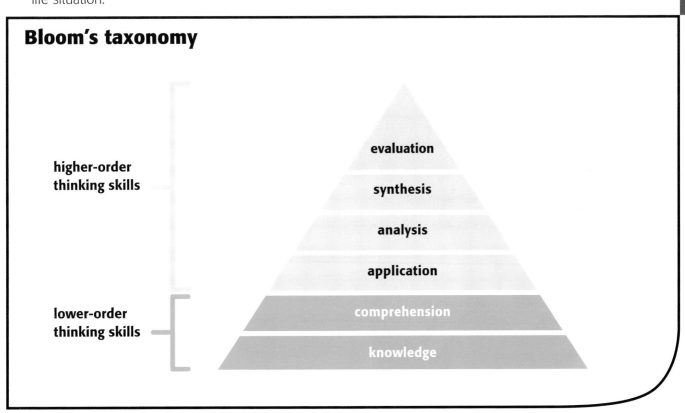

Bloom's taxonomy

higher-order thinking skills

- evaluation
- synthesis
- analysis
- application

lower-order thinking skills

- comprehension
- knowledge

Then the learner combines this idea with ones they already know and they can then evaluate the theory, knowledge or skills in different situations.

We learn things on different levels and in different ways. We want learners to demonstrate learning because in that way we know they have mastery. This idea is at the heart of training where it is often abbreviated to knowledge, skills and attitude. The process of acquiring knowledge, skills and attitutes is similar.

case study

William is a lecturer in Marketing within a further education college.

'As far as formal training is concerned I took a degree when I was in my early 20s. I was working on a building site and was not happy with being in a dead-end job. I got a 2:2 in my degree, and then tried teaching. After a year I took a postgraduate teaching course, but when I finished I could not get a job. This is where experience starts. I went into sales and became the marketing director of a medium-sized company in the photographic industry. In the recession of the early 1980s, however, we did not survive and I was made redundant. I wanted to work and put my excellent experience into action. I eventually got some part-time work at a local college and that led to a full-time job. I keep up to date with the employers panel I have developed, and with doing frequent spells of work experience in marketing and advertising, which are the subjects I teach at foundation degree level. I have also studied for and got marketing qualifications. I think I am in the right job now.'

chapter 3 **teaching in your specialist area**

activity

Break William's background into phases. How relevant is his experience for the job he teaches? How important are his formal qualifications for his teaching? To what extent is he in a better position to teach compared with a marketing graduate who has had no formal teacher training? How does he keep up to date? Record in notes or draw a mind map of how to keep up to date.

What makes you think that you are qualified? Draw up a curriculum vitae (CV) – a list of your qualifications and experience – you can and will use for applying for jobs, training or as a teacher.

Don't forget to include all the relevant experience in details, references and referees who can support what you say. Referees should usually be people who either are ex-employers or are professional people of standing such as teachers, lawyers or doctors. Include any commendations you have received that are relevant to your future applications and any prizes that you have won in your career. Also include anything that shows how you have been able to keep up to date in your area such as training courses.

William's CV is shown on page 42. It will give you some ideas of format.

There are many different ways of setting out a CV. There are many books that suggest alternatives and there are also many websites offering advice. The important thing to remember is there is no set way of doing it. It is something that will change constantly with your career and experience. Many people also change their CV to suit the situation or job that they are applying for.

CV template

William Harris
143 Chatsworth Road
Rugby
Warwickshire
RG90 9XY

mob: 09209 909090

email: will@harris.net.uk

tel: 00700 700700

A natural leader who is popular with both his peers and students. Highly organised and able to use initiative when coping with difficult and demanding situations.

D.O.B. 14 April 1953

QUALIFICATIONS

7 GCSEs	English, Maths, IT, Science, French, Business Studies, PE	1966
3 A-levels	English, Business Studies, Physical Education	1968
BSc Business & Marketing	London University	1973
Post-Graduate Certificate in Education	Birmingham University	1976
CAM Diploma in Marketing Communications	Valencia University, Spain	1977

NON-TEACHING POSTS

Photowaste Ltd, London   October 1978 – August 1984
● Salesman for South East England from 1978 to 1980
Promoted to Head Salesperson in 1980, responsible for managing team of three salespeople – ensuring the team achieved ambitious sales targets.
● Sales Manager for Eastern Region from 1981 to 1984
Managed three teams. Main responsibilities included ensuring all sales targets met and developing individual potential within the team.

TEACHING POSTS

West Midlands College, Leamington Spa   September 1994 to date
● Curriculum Team Leader. Responsibilities included developing materials, supervising the teaching team, carrying out lesson observations and organising curriculum changes.
West Herts College, Watford   August 1990 to July 1994
● Further Education Lecturer. Delivered HND and BTEC National Marketing courses. Responsible for creating schemes of work.
Croydon College, Croydon   September 1984 to July 1990
● Part-time Further Education Lecturer. Taught BTEC Business and Marketing courses.

INTERESTS AND ACTIVITIES

Prior to commencing full-time employment in 1978, undertook work shadowing at an advertising agency and a computing trader
Captain of local football team from 1986 to 1993
Currently referee for local football league

REFERENCES   Will be supplied on request

summary

In this chapter we learnt about teaching in your specialist area. We learnt how essential it is to keep up to date. We discovered that teaching in your specialist area can involve unusual skills, which need to be developed separately from the rest of the training for learners. We learnt that teaching in your area needs a thorough knowledge of teaching and training and may also use special skills that sometimes involve unusual learning styles, such as touch, taste and smell. We discovered that teaching is not only passing on information, it involves mastery of skills and the ability to use the knowledge in different situations. We learnt the importance of knowledge, skills and attitude. You drew up a CV and geared it towards your teaching. We discussed the importance of observing an experienced teacher in your area deliver a session. We thought about what we should looking for when observing other teachers and what this can tell us. We considered the importance of skills, the sort of skills we use in our jobs and our specialist area. We discussed the importance of learners mastering basic skills. We saw how to put basic skills into our specialist area.

Resources

Bloom, B.S. (1956) *Taxonomy of Educational Objectives: Handbook 1* New York: Longman.

www.totallyskilled.org.uk.

www.ofsted.gov.uk.

Preparing to Teach

In this chapter, I have learnt about:

- ☐ Keeping up to date
- ☐ Unusual skills in your area
- ☐ Unusual learning styles
- ☐ An introduction to Bloom
- ☐ Knowledge, skills and attitude
- ☐ A CV for teaching
- ☐ Observing a teacher or trainer
- ☐ A checklist to use
- ☐ Learning skills
- ☐ Skills in our area
- ☐ Embedding common skills

planning
and planning skills

subject

In this chapter you will learn the importance of plans, demonstrate session planning skills and choosing resources.

learning outcomes

In this chapter you will learn how to:

■ **Plan a teaching and learning session which meets the needs of individual** learners.
Assessment criteria 3.1

■ **Justify a selection of resources for a specific session.**
Assessment criteria 3.2

study skills

time management

theme

Study skills

Some people are always on time. Annoying isn't it? Well it shouldn't be. Think realistically about your time management skills. How good are you at time management? Do you always arrive on time? Are you always early? Are you always late? How could you improve your time management and thus your organisation skills?

Napoleon said, 'It is a wise man who makes plans and it is a fool who sticks to them.' Planning is essential in life and work, it is about being prepared, being in control, being positive, thinking in advance, thinking things through, time management and, especially for Napoleon, leading. Napoleon realised the importance of all these things and also the need to leave room for spontaneity and the unexpected. In teaching we need to be aware that things can occur for which we haven't planned, however without plans we are lost. The worst feeling in the world is to be in front of a group of learners when you have run out of things to do and there is still half an hour to go to the end of the session. Completing on time feels good, feels in control and leaves you satisfied, ready to continue with the programme.

Planning in teaching has several aspects. Short-term planning, such as lesson plans, is for individual sessions and considers the needs of individual learners. Medium-term planning looks at meeting targets and it includes a healthy section of review and analysis, in-course evaluations and meeting the goals for the course and the goals for individuals. Long-term planning for the whole course is when overall objectives are taken into account, and final assessments are included. This type of planning is often called schemes of work in teaching, and proposals in training. In teaching we usually start with the long term and work towards the individual session.

Top tips

Reflection

Think of a meeting you attended or led that was arranged at short notice with no time for you to prepare. Analyse your experience. What came out of the meeting that you felt was positive? What did you learn?

chapter 4 **planning and planning skills**

Barney is a lecturer in the construction department of a Further Education college. He has been teaching for more than 10 years, since qualifying as a teacher through a full-time course in a London training college. Before that he worked as a painter, having done an apprenticeship with a decorator after leaving school. He has a wealth of experience and uses anecdotes and real life stories in every class.

'I find it helps and I like to have a laugh with the kids I am teaching. The thing I found trickiest when I first started teaching was planning. Not so much what I would do from day to day, but how I would do things over the year. In other words, writing a scheme of work. Once I got down to it, it wasn't as bad as I thought, and plenty of people helped me out. The organisation that produces the tests tells you what you've got to cover. A scheme of work tells the college and the learners when you will do sessions and a lesson plan tells you how. It is like painting a house. You don't start with a bit of gloss on the bathroom door frame. You have to prepare and fill, sand and sand. Preparation is everything. The finish comes at the end and you have to get everything in place before. I didn't realise it but we used a scheme of work for every job I had. We always stuck to it as well.'

activity

Demonstrate three goals that you have set yourself for the end of this month. If you are already teaching, they could be goals you have established in the classroom. If you are not teaching, then they should be work related. Show how you will achieve your goals. You have five minutes to do this task. How you demonstrate this is up to you, but it must be to at least one other person.

RPJ

Neil and Irene run a croquet primer for beginners. The course consists of six lessons and the aim is to get complete novices ready to play association croquet. They have been following this plan since August 2002. Irene thought it was successful:

'We have introduced a hundred or more people to the game since we started. Many are keen players. From the start we realised how important it was to plan our sessions. We used the wisdom our teachers had passed on to us many years ago and met with the committees of the clubs in the county league to establish what was essential, in their opinion, to cover. We believe the scheme has been so successful because we listened to all those involved in croquet before the scheme was launched. It has stood the test of time, a little tweaking here and there based on the advice of those who completed the course but otherwise it is consistent. Croquet is a game that has changed very little over the years.'

The session plans look like this:

Session 1 - Court and equipment, mallets and balls, stance, grip, swing, single ball shots. Running straight hoops, running angled hoops, push and crush shots, yard-lines and baulk-lines. Hoops in order. Introduction to golf croquet.

Session 2 – Croquet, straight croquet shots – drive, stop and roll. Split croquet stroke – an introduction

Session 3 – Split croquet stroke – more detail. Hoop approach. Thin take off. Three hoop break using take offs. Use of clips.

Session 4 – Four ball break. Bisques

Session 5 – Straight rush. Cut rush. Rush set up from yard-line breaks. Rush lines.

Session 6 – Start of game. 14 point game.

activity

Identify the strong points of the plan developed by Irene and Neil. What are the areas you would suggest they could develop?

In teaching lesson plans have an agreed form, there are things that have developed over the years and are always included by agreement. Within post-school education, we suggest that a plan is laid out according to the teacher. However, the essential things that should be included are listed right.

At some point, you should include a brief description of the group, for example, the number on the register and a one-line description, such as 14–18-year-olds excluded from school. You should also have some idea of what skills and knowledge the learners have before you meet them.

You should show how you are incorporating differentiation and equal opportunities – making allowances for learners with learning issues and presenting information fairly. You will need to demonstrate how different needs are being met at each stage of the session.

Lession plans should also cover:

- Context of session – for example, working with percentages

- Session aims and learning outcomes – what a learner can do and understand as a result of learning. What the learners will be able to do as a result of the session.

- Session plan(s) – including an appreciation of timings

- What the learners will be expected to do during the session

- What the teacher will do during the session (usually this will be a variety of things)

- Materials to support teaching and learning – in other words, the resources required

- The assessment method – how you will determine what the learners have learnt

- Evaluation of session – this is the reflective practice that a teacher uses everyday and with every session

- Evidence of embedding skills where appropriate

- In addition, it is usually possible to link the session into the overall scheme, and show where extra work is expected and how it will be followed up.

- The date

- The time – be sure to stick to this

- The location – in details, people will want to come and see you

- Duration

- The course – the details and the name of the organisation that supervises it

- The title of the lesson – the topic

Preparing to Teach

 Lesson planning

Justify a selection of resources for a specific session.

Assessment criteria 3.2

One of the most influential ideas in modern teaching and learning comes from David Kolb (1984). Kolb's learning cycle divides learning into layers. He states that in the 'doing part' of a lesson or training session the learner undertakes a task, they then reflect or think about what they have done. They will then consider whether there are other ways of undertaking the task (an opportunity to compare and contrast). Finally, they do the task again from a position backed by new experience and understanding.

This is the basis of most adult and continuing education lessons. It is often known as experiential learning. You need to allow learners to undertake tasks so that they can reinforce their learning through reflection.

Kolb's learning cycle

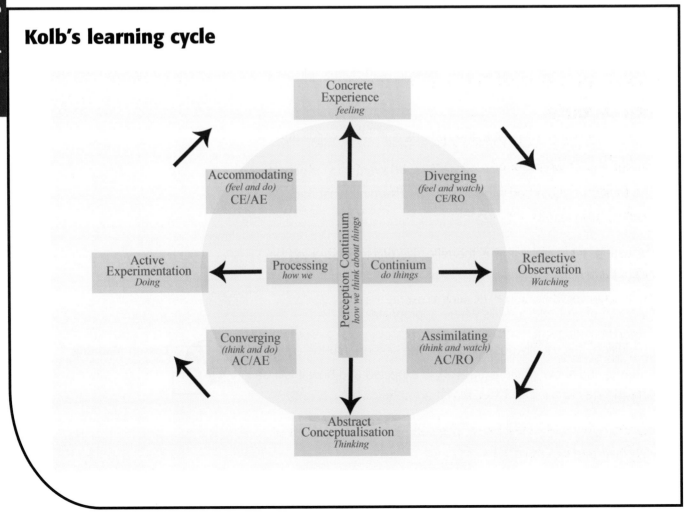

activity

Use an appropriate way to show how the concept of experiential learning (the circular pattern of learning from experience, through reflection and conceptualisation to action and so onto further experience) can be used in the teaching of your subject.

To allow learners to experiment and learn by doing we need to provide the right conditions and tools for learning to take place. For an IT group, for example, we need to ensure that learners have a room with computers in it. For a course on flying, we need to ensure that learners and trainers have access to flight simulators.

activity

Make a list of the resources you would like, in an ideal world, to introduce the first session in your chosen subject. How they should be arranged – a purpose built room? an ordinary classroom? a training suite?

It is important that learners are in the right location with the correct tools. It also makes a difference how we arrange the layout of the room.

Room layouts

There are no hard and fast rules about layout and teachers need to experiment – what works for one group may not for another and each has its strengths. Purpose-built facilities are harder as their layout is usually fixed. Layouts include:

- The traditional front-facing rows where the whole group can see the instructor or teacher. The learners at the back are more remote and the teacher has difficulty in reaching those furthest away.

- The horseshoe shape with the trainer at the centre and equidistant from the learners.

- Similarly the semi-circle layout, which is centred on the teacher.

- Islands, or pods, are ideal for small group work where learners sit with their backs to the teacher.

Consider the different layout options for a group session. Make notes on how this could affect group dynamics, the way the class interacts with the teacher and with each other. Did it make a difference when you tried other layouts? What layout worked best and why do you think that was?

It is the teacher's responsibility to ensure that learning is supported with the right resources, and that resources are of a high quality and meet the subject and the learners' needs. Before preparing for a session you should consider the policies of your organisation, and how they apply to you. You also need to consider issues relating to health and safety in the classroom or training room environment, and current regional and national standards. This is extremely important in learning sessions covering areas such as the construction industry or hospitality.

Skills input

Timing is a difficult skill that is essential if you want the session to go well. There is no trick; good time-keeping is a discipline that requires careful observance of watches and clocks. A plan, of course, helps. A general rule is that each lesson should have three parts, like a play or a film: a beginning, a middle and an end or conclusion. A lesson that does not introduce the subject and put it into perspective does not work. The session that stops suddenly rather than being drawn to a conclusion leaves things hanging in the air. It is important therefore to ensure that all sessions have all three components. Try to make sure that your lessons or sessions always do.

Tony is a pastry chef. He was employed by a major luxury hotel chain as a head chef. Pastries are his area of speciality. He is preparing for a two-hour lesson on the first-year professional chef's course in which the learners will tackle choux pastry for the first time. The outcome will be that the learners will produce profiteroles, which will then be sold in the college refectory if the chef approves of them. If they are not up to standard then the products will not be sold.

The ingredients that Tony will be using are water, butter, flour and eggs. The cost of these ingredients is met by the course budget.

The method he uses is the same he used when he was in charge of the kitchens at the hotel chain. As you read the recipe and the actions set out below, try to work out what resources learners will need for the session. Tony will assess the quality of the pastry and only if he is satified will it be baked. The session is timetabled for two hours.

1. Preheat over to 190° to 205°C

2. Melt the butter in the water and bring to a full boil.

3. Immediately add the flour all at once and stir continuously with a wooden spoon.

4. Cook for a couple of minutes until the mixture pulls away from the pan, forming a ball, and remove from the heat.

5. Place the dough in a bowl or a mixer. Using a wooden spoon or the paddle attachment, mix the dough for a few minutes, allowing it to cool slightly.

6. Add the beaten eggs gradually, in three or four additions, mixing the dough until it is smooth each time. Scrape down the sides and bottom of the bowl until all of the eggs are incorporated. The paste should be of a pipeable consistency.

7. Pipe the dough into shapes, onto baking sheets lined with baking paper, allowing space for them to raise and expand.

8. Place into a pre-heated oven, on the middle shelf: begin the baking process at a high temp. (190° to 205°C) and allow to bake for 20 minutes. Then reduce the heat to 120°C and continue to bake until they turn golden brown and crisp.

activity

Preparing to Teach

Assuming that Tony has access to a teaching kitchen of the right size for his group of first-year professional chefs, what resources would he need for this session? Draft a lesson plan for this session. Use the information you have learnt about time management. Ensure that there is a section marked resources which details the things he will need to complete the task and allow the learners to achieve the competencies.

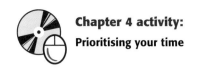
In a session like that described on page 53, time management is very important. It is a mirror of the real world. In a restaurant, dishes have to be prepared in a given time. Customers will not be satisfied if the food is slow to arrive; the training kitchen tries to recreate the same sense of deadline.

activity

Create a timetable for your working week.

Study skill – time management

The first rule of time management is planning. Without accurate plans pressure will mount. This chapter is all about planning and aims to address this. The list, bottom left, provides some useful tips.

Problems will always occur; the value of a good plan is to identify them early and seek out solutions. Good time management enables you to measure progress towards your goals and what you can measure, you can control. Always try to be proactive. It is worthwhile researching time management. There is a wealth of information about it on the Internet and a great number of books have been written on the subject.

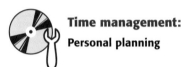

Time management:
Personal planning

- Analyse your use of time
- Being organised is important
- Make sure that you assess at the beginning of the year, the work that is expected of you
- Know your deadline dates and work towards them. This is what a scheme of work or a training proposal is all about
- Identify a goal and then work towards it
- Always be in control, never let things get on top of you. Manage your time as best you can, this means keeping

case study

Sarah is running a half-day training session on stress in the workplace. She introduces the topic and asks the 10 learners to talk about at least one time when stress took over their lives and they found it difficult to do their job properly. Sarah tries to be flexible and not stick too rigidly to a planned programme. By the time lunch comes, the eighth learner is still speaking about the problems of the stress he felt from the day before. The session is closed. By the afternoon her client, the human resources manager at the company, tells Sarah he is not renewing her contract, even though the staff who took part said how much they enjoyed the session. Comments included: 'A good chance to let off steam and I felt less stressed by the end … it was a great bonding session.' They also complimented Sarah on her pleasant and unobtrusive style.

What went wrong? Do you feel the human resources manager was right to terminate her contract? How could Sarah have delivered the session so that all the learners and the HR manager were happy?

summary

In this chapter we learnt about the importance of planning and how preparation is an essential part of teaching. We discussed and saw how timing is critical, and that all teachers or trainers need to keep a careful eye on timing when they are delivering a session. Remember what Napoleon said and plan, but always leave room for spontaneity and for issues that may arise. The skills theme of the chapter was time management.

Resources

Kolb, D. (1984) *Experiential Learning: Experience as the Source of Learning and Development* Upper Saddle River, NJ: Prentice Hall.

In this chapter, I have learnt about:

- ☐ Planning theory
- ☐ Planning practice
- ☐ Time management theory
- ☐ Time management practice
- ☐ Schemes of work and training proposals

- ☐ Session plans
- ☐ The learning cycle (after Kolb)
- ☐ The importance of variety
- ☐ The importance of humour
- ☐ The importance of understanding individual learners

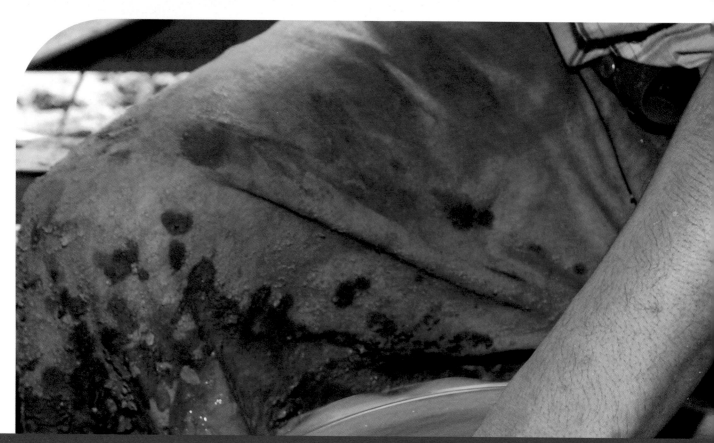

inclusive learning

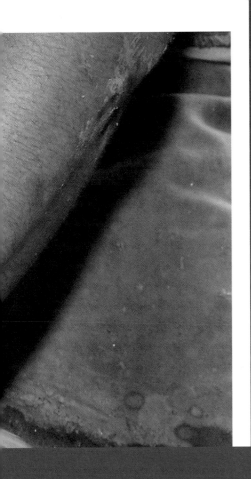

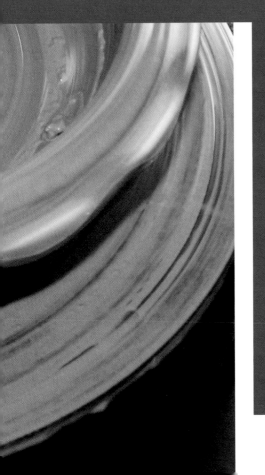

subject

Inclusive learning.

learning outcomes

In this chapter you will learn how to:

- Explain ways to establish ground rules with learners that underpin appropriate behaviour and respect for others.

  Assessment criteria 4.1

- Use a range of appropriate and effective teaching and learning approaches to engage and motivate learners in your teaching or training.

  Assessment criteria 4.2

- Explain and demonstrate good practice in giving feedback.

  Assessment criteria 4.3

- Communicate appropriately and effectively with learners.

  Assessment criteria 4.4

- Reflect on and evaluate the effectiveness of your own teaching.

  Assessment criteria 4.5

study skills

commu-
nication

theme

Explain ways to establish ground rules with learners that underpin appropriate behaviour and respect for others.

Assessment criteria 4.1

Ice-breakers

You will find ice-breakers invaluable. It is a good idea to get to know your group straight away, and to encourage them to communicate with each other. If you are new to the group, try to start with an ice-breaker. There are many ice-breakers available on the Internet, in text books and on the CD-ROM in the front of this book.

Here are a few examples:

- Divide the group into pairs and ask them to interview each other. Ask the interviewer to report back to the group about the person they have interviewed. Subjects that could be covered might include: the learner's background; why they are taking this course or training session; their best learning experience; how they came to it and what they want to get out of it. (This information will be useful for you as it could help you to learn about your learner's motivation.) We will discuss motivation in more detail later in this chapter.

- Divide the learners into small groups (three or four per group). Ask them to discuss their own backgrounds in training, and to talk about one session they found helpful – their best training. Get a spokesperson to report back to the group as a whole, drawing out themes from the reports. This activity should give you some additional information about learning styles and attitudes.

- If there is only one learner, talk to them and find out about their background and their reasons for taking the course.

- It is always a good idea for you to tell the group about yourself at the start. It breaks the ice and establishes your standing and your expertise.

Once you have broken the ice with the group and they have gotten to know each other, it is a good opportunity to establish some ground rules.

chapter 5 **inclusive learning**

'I teach ICT and have found it very useful to get learners to send me a 'Dear Pat' letter via email during the first session of the course. While all of the learners are sitting in front of their computers and logged-on, I ask them to fire up the internal mail system and send me a short email with their name, brief background, previous ICT experience and expectations of the course. This serves many functions; they get to know the email system, I take the roll, I collect information on the general skill level of the class, etc. Perhaps most importantly they get the idea that email is a good way to communicate with me. Using this exercise I have increased email communications from classes from half a dozen per semester to about that many per week.'

Within further and higher education, it is usual for the learners to be interviewed and tested prior to the start of the course, often by the teacher themselves. This pre-testing can be done by another unit, for example the Admissions unit or Advice and Guidance department. The teacher can then access this information before the start of the first lesson.

activity

Research and observe an Advice and Guidance unit at work. Use notes or a mind map to explain your findings to at least one other person.

Preparing to Teach

The following is taken from a sheet given out to learners at the start of a football coaching course.

Level 1 Coaching Certificate in Football

All courses are based on having fun, it's a great chance to meet new team-mates and friends and also improve your football skills at the same time with some of the best coaches around – there's also a free gift and certificate for all those that attend, plus the chance to win a medal.

The courses will offer professional football tuition to both boys and girls, aged between five and 18, for over four hours a day providing local youngsters with the chance to play and learn about football while having lots of fun.

The skills learnt whilst on the course range from dribbling to defending, with the groups able to put these skills into practice during a knock out 'World Cup' tournament held on the final day.

There are five sessions of one to two hours per session.

Sessions begin at 10.30 a.m. prompt each Wednesday with a briefing, so please arrive in good time.

If you can not attend a session please telephone one of the coaches in advance.

Health and safety warning

Grass banks can be slippery especially when wet. Please take extra care on the way to pitches. Take care to avoid tripping over or stepping on equipment which is left at the sides of pitches. The main door to the pavilion may be low for some people. The decking around the pavilion may be slippery. Please take soccer boots off before entering the pavilion. Soccer is a contact sport and some injuries are inevitable but please follow sensible practice and try to keep these injuries to a minimum. The authority take no responsibility for participants who do not follow these rules.

activity

What are the strengths of this course information sheet? What things are not covered that you think should be?

Develop and present a short leaflet introducing your course to a group of learners.

Organisations will have their own rules and procedures and learners can be referred to these. However, it is good to get things straight from the start. Depending on the situation, these can be presented simply by talking through a few ground rules about acceptable behaviour, teacher's expectations, attendance and punctuality. This needs to be agreed at the first meeting, and perhaps reviewed as the group come to know each other better. However, in many situations, health and safety regulations may mean that rules must be covered in more detail, and learners be reminded of them during the course. For example, where hazardous materials are involved in a chemistry session. With many groups it is useful to have them tell you what they consider the rules should be, and to establish the rules by agreement. This may include what is acceptable behaviour, the responsibilities of the learners and those of the teacher. The teacher should lead this session.

Reflection
Comment on this list and the usefulness of this exercise. What are your own rules for studying?

activity

Establish a list of ground rules for a group of learners. This could be the group you are involved withon this course.

activity

Imagine you have overall responsibility for the New Day Project Group. How would you establish ground rules for this challenging and testing group ? What should be covered by these ground rules?

Group contract

Use a range of appropirate and effective teaching and learning approaches to engage and motivate learners in your teaching or training.

Assessment criteria 4.2

Motivation is a topic close to the hearts of most teachers and trainers. Unless learners are motivated they won't perform to the best of their abilities. Herzberg (1959) was the first to show that satisfaction and dissatisfaction were nearly always caused by different things.

His work followed the work of Maslow (1943), who suggested that people are always needing something and what they need depends upon what they already have. Their needs can be arranged in a series of levels. When they have achieved their needs at one level they move on to the next level.

Maslow suggested five levels (see below right). You should read Maslow and Herzberg to come to an understanding of what motivates people.

Herzberg's motivational factors

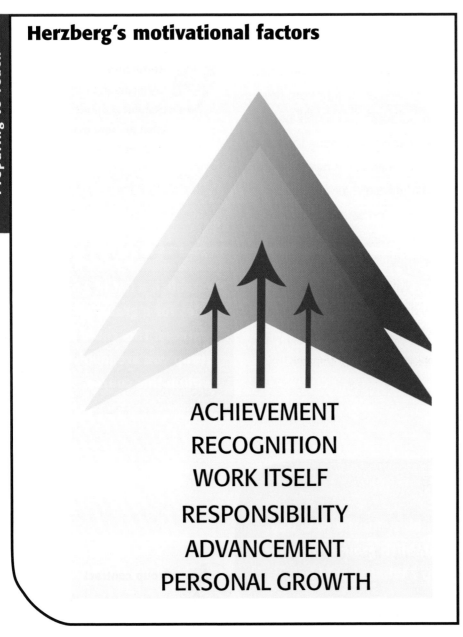

ACHIEVEMENT
RECOGNITION
WORK ITSELF
RESPONSIBILITY
ADVANCEMENT
PERSONAL GROWTH

Physiological needs – These are our basic needs: the desire to satisfy hunger and thirst, the need for oxygen and sleep, among others.

Safety needs – These are the need to feel safe and secure, be free from pain and threats.

Social needs – This is the need for a sense of family, belonging and friendship.

Esteem needs – This is the need for self-respect and self-confidence, and the desire to be recognised by others.

Self-actualisation needs – This is the need to achieve what you think you are capable of, either a physical act or a state of mind. It means different things to different people.

chapter 5 **inclusive learning**

How does this apply to teachers? Herzberg's research shows that people will strive to satisfy basic needs (which he calls hygiene factors) because they are dissatisfied if these needs are not fulfilled. True motivators were found to be other completely different things, such as: achievement, recognition, work itself, responsibility, advancement and personal growth. Despite what is commonly thought, money is only a motivator if it allows people to achieve their basic needs or ambitions.

Recent research has shown the following to be important:

Enthusiasm. Enthusiasm is infectious and learners say that what impresses them the most is the enthusiasm of teachers.

Feedback. Give frequent, early, positive feedback as it encourages learners to believe that they can do well.

Opportunitites to succeed. Make certain there are chances for learners to succeed by assigning tasks that are neither too easy nor too difficult.

Meaning and value. Help learners find meaning and value in the material.

Atmosphere. Create an atmosphere that is open and positive.

Status. Help learners feel they are valued members of a learning community.

Good teaching practice. Good everyday teaching practices can do more to counter learner apathy than special efforts to promote motivation.

Relevance. Learners react better if they can see the point of learning, and how it links in to the bigger picture. It is always good practice at the start of a session for you to link the session to the bigger context: how it fits into the scheme, to the wider picture and to their qualification in particular.

Involvement. Learners learn by doing, making, writing, designing, creating and solving. If they are not asked to take part they switch off.

Drawing on previous knowledge. Don't tell learners something when you could ask them

Some other motivational ideas are:

Get learners to put forward their own ideas to solve a problem.

Frame your theories in real-life contexts, ones to which learners can relate.

Hold high but realistic expectations for your learners.

 Top tips

Help learners set achievable goals for themselves.

Tell learners what they need to do to succeed in your course.

Strengthen learner self-motivation.

Avoid creating intense competition between learners.

case study

Bob is an experienced teacher who has worked, part time, for many years teaching physics to a variety of learners of different ages and abilities.

Bob is very enthusiastic and knows his subject thoroughly. He is very aware of the pressures of the syllabus and the need to get the work covered. Because of this, he finds that he has to spend all his time in class giving the learners the information that he feels they need in order to pass the exams at the end of the course. The information takes the form of duplicated sheets, from which the learners are expected to extract the data, and lectures where the learners are given notes, either through dictation or written on the board.

The learners are mainly 16–18-years-olds on the first or second year of their two-year A-level course. They have attained at least five GCSE passes with decent grades – including English, maths and physics or science. Although they have GCSE English their working vocabulary is limited – a fact not actually recognised by Bob who assumes they follow what he says! Bob asks questions of the learners and attempts to get discussions going, but the learners do not join in and display very poor motivation.

Work is set now and again, but not regularly, and is not always collected in. Therefore most of the learners begin to fall behind with their assignments, feeling that they are optional! The work that is handed in is done piecemeal, it is not returned regularly and learners may have to wait long periods of time before marked work is returned. When they do get marked work back, comments are written on it that the learners can't understand.

activity

Wat is going wrong in this scenario? Suggest a solution that will help Bob to motivate his learners. What effect do you think this may also have on Bob's own motivation?

A session usually falls into three parts, and each part is equally important.

An introduction is essential for every session as it starts each session on an even footing. First greet the learners, by name, if possible (in an HE group of over 50 it may not be), making them feel welcome. Give an overview of the session: the aims, the expected outcomes, what activities will be included and how learning will be judged. Link the session to others, especially any previous sessions and briefly summarise the learning. Use questioning to check on the knowledge and previous experiences of the learners. A case study may be helpful.

In the second, or development phase, use a variety of strategies to keep the learners involved and to allow them to learn using their own preferred style.

The last phase should assess how the session has gone. Before the session finishes, draw everything together, review the lesson and give the learners feedback. It is also a good time to hear how the session went for them. Learning should never take place in isolation, this is a great opportunity to link the session to the overall plan, the other things the learners may be studying and the next session. Outline any work that the learners will need to do to follow up this session, and how they can prepare for the next session. Finally, allow time for the learners to clear away any equipment and their paperwork. Assessment of learning will be covered in detail in Chapter 6. In Chapter 5 we will talk about the different ways that we can judge what learners have taken from our session.

When running a session, it is important to add variety so that all learners can get maximum value from the session. Learning is meant to be enjoyable, and the introduction of humour is a good thing. Even when the subject is serious there will be chances for light moments in all sessions. Try to give learners variety in the way that information and skills are presented to them.

In Chapter 2 we saw how we all differ in our response to information and that we all have a favoured learning style. It is sensible to think about learners as individuals with their own demands and strengthsand to present information in a variety of ways. Do this and the group will enjoy your sessions and get the maximum from them.

There are a number of different ways of delivering sessions. They can be delivered to individual learners, to small groups or to large groups. In the same way learners can work on their own or as part of a team.

Preparing to Teach

When planning sessions we should consider what the learners need and want from the sessions. We should think of the skills they need, their attitudes and the dynamics of the group as a whole.

activity

Prepare a lesson for a group of learners. This could be a group that you already teach or train. Use any information and knowledge that you have about your group.

Your session should last for about one hour, or 20 minutes if you ar epresenting to a micro teaching group. Make the timings within your sessions as accurate as possible.

the subject is up to you, it can be the subject you want to teach or something that you are intested in, know and love. how you present the session plan is again up to you, but, it should contain all the important things discussed earlier in this chapter

chapter 5 **inclusive learning**

Explain and demonstrate good practice in giving feedback.

When we have assessed learners throughout a course, what do we do with the information? At the end of the course when we collect marks, how do we tell learners how they performed?

The answer is through accurate feedback. Feedback is very helpful in establishing a good working relationship with learners. Experienced teachers will tell you it is an essential tool, but it does have to be used wisely.

Feedback can be motivational, but given in the wrong way it can have the opposite effect. The traditional method is to return work marked with comments from the teacher, and this usually works well. It has advantages: there is a record of the assessment, the learner and the marker can agree on the outcome and it can be recorded. Asking learners questions about the topic is an instant way of assessing how well the session has gone and a way of discovering instantly if your learners have truly grasped information. The issue, however, is that learners have very little say in this type of feedback. Oral feedback can be used to supplement marked work, the teacher can tell the learner what they thought of the work and what they believe the learner should do next. This option allows the learner to react and negotiate grades based on the evidence. Beware however, this can require tact; learners are sensitive. A common way of providing feedback is the personal tutorial, where the information exchange is confidential.

Preparing to Teach

case study

Graham is an inexperienced teacher of Finance in his first year of teaching. He takes a group of GCE first-year students. After the second week, he decides that the students should take a test to allow him to gauge their progress, and how they have performed so far on the course. The results are varied.

How would you suggest that Graham gives the marks to individual students? What issues do you think he should be aware of before he gives feedback to the students? What would be the value of this type of formative assessment?

RPJ

Feedback is an excellent chance for us to do some informal formative assessment of individual learners.

Some general suggestions for successful feedback are:

- Feedback should be clear. This means easy to understand chunks of information.

- Feedback should be owned, sharing ideas rather than giving advice. 'I thought … I felt'.

- Feedback should be positive and negative. It may be difficult to find anything wrong with a piece of work and that is commendable, but it is the exception.

- A useful technique to use is the 'sandwich theory'. Start oral feedback with a positive reaction to the piece of work. Always finish with something else up-beat, any criticisms are 'sandwiched' in between. This tends to be a much more balanced and motivational way of passing on the same ideas.

- Feedback should be realistic. Any goals set as the result of the feedback should be achievable.

- Feedback should be negotiable. You should allow the learner opportunities to explain their reaction.

- Feedback should be specific, not general.

- Have a time limit on feedback sessions.

case study

Helena teaches Political Philosophy at a university in London. When she returns learners' work she always does it within the allotted two weeks standard for her department. The learner's work is returned with a script, often over two pages long in which she seemingly analyses every phrase. The grades she gives are strictly non-negotiable and the learners are not allowed to discuss them with her after they have received the marks.

What do you feel about this method of feedback? Can you see any problems that could occur as a result of this method of feedback?

chapter 5 **inclusive learning**

Identify a learner that you have had experience of teaching or a learner featured in this text. Prepare notes for a feedback session with them following a test designed to find out their progress so far on the course. Deliver this feedback to another person, but do not identify the student by name. Discuss what the other person felt about your feedback.

Reflection

How effective do you feel this feedback was? Did you get over the things that you wanted to? Were there things that occurred you had not planned for? How will you develop these skills as a result of this rehearsal?

case study

Lara teaches People in Organisations, a unit in the travel and tourism foundation degree at a Midlands college. She tries to incorporate a variety of styles in her sessions.

'I try to cater for all learners: visual with diagrams and PowerPoint presentations; auditory with discussions and role plays as well as more formal lecture type inputs; and kinaesthetic, encouraging them to take notes, role-plays, doing things and computer work.'

When it comes to feedback she has an unusual method of returning work.

'With the assignments, this is the work that helps me support the learners, tells me how they're doing, and it contributes to their final grades. Feedback is a vital part of my relationship with the individuals. When I give the marked work back, I do so in individual sessions that are timed at five minute intervals. I have my own records and I dictate my feelings and opinions to the students who write them down on the front cover of the work. We agree a grade – theirs is usually one grade lower than mine – and we both sign and date the record. There is no negotiation afterwards. The learners seem to feel it is a fair system.'

How do you feel about this system? Do you feel it works for the individuals? Does it involve extra work for the teacher? What are the strengths of this system of feedback? In what ways do you feel Lara's method could be improved? Draw a mind map that you would use to present your findings to your teaching group or to another interested party.

Preparing to Teach

Communicate appropriately and effectively with learners.

Skills input

Communication is defined as the act or process of transmitting information. It is essential and is what teaching is all about. Shannon and Weaver (1949) produced a model that reduces communication to a process of 'transmitting information'. It is a tried and tested model that has been found to work very well in the classroom.

The model consists of five elements:

- An information source, the teacher of the learner who produces a message.

- A transmitter, which encodes the message into signals, usually by thinking what would be the most effective form and content for that situation.

- A channel, the way the message is sent, and in what form. It could be by talking or it could be an actual transmission, such as by television.

- A receiver, which could be the ears or the eyes of the learner.

- A destination, where the message arrives. Feedback can be used to check that the recipient understands.

Noise is any interference with the message travelling along the channel (such as static on the telephone or radio, or typically in teaching when learners do not listen). This can lead to the signal received being different from that sent. It follows that a teacher who mumbles, who swallows words, who speaks in a monotonous manner, who delivers unexplained technical and specialist terms, who does not repeat points and speaks too quickly, will be less effective.

There are also non-verbal barriers to communication. For example, a teacher needs to have the right appearance – a suit used to be the standard, now it is smart casual dress. Learners may prefer a more informal dress style, but if this is too scruffy and you might look as if you don't care or aren't professional. Poor eye contact in our culture is felt to show a degree of nervousness and can indicate disinterest.

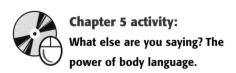 **Chapter 5 activity:**
What else are you saying? The power of body language.

Reflect on and evaluate the effectiveness of your own teaching?

Assessment criteria 4.5

Reflection is the second stage in the learning cycle. It is about estimating your own performance and has been a theme in this text throughout. The idea that we can learn from what we do is something that is very basic in teaching or training. Teachers usually keep a diary where they log the learners' performance and make notes about things such as:

- What went well?

- What did the learners find difficult and what tactics did I use?

- Were all the learners successful?

- If not, which learners were not and how might I reach them next time?

Reflection
In what ways can you use communication theory in your lessons to help motivate your learners? In what ways is communication different between small and large groups? Or say for students who are disabled and are wheelchair users?

case studies

Freddie has been profoundly deaf since birth. He has fought his way through the system and has achieved six GCSE passes. He is anxious not to allow his disability to stand in his way and wants to go to university. He is doing a BTEC National in Business to allow him to do this. The unit we are looking at is one that focuses on Marketing and the scheduled session is the third in the programme. The theme of the session is principles, and applying the principle of getting the right product to the right place at the right time, with the right promotion. The second theme to be introduced is the product life cycle.

What issues would the teacher face for this lesson with Freddie? What suggestions do you have for ways of presenting the information to the group? How would you present the information and ensure that Freddie is included as a learner?

Martin is teaching a group of 16–19-year-old adult learners taking a sports instructors course. He takes them for ICT and the session is delivered on Friday afternoons at 3.00 p.m. He finds it hard as the group is often switched off by then.

What ways can you suggest for him to introduce a topic like communication theory to the group that gets a response and gets them active and involved in this difficult teaching slot?

How did the group respond to different activities?

What styles of presenting information were particularly effective?

What things went badly?

How could I improve what I did this time to make it even more effective next time?

What materials were particularly helpful and what did not work?

Why was this?

Did the lesson start and finish on time?

If I taught the lesson again what would I do that was different?

 RPJ

Other ways we have of helping with reflection could be to record a session. Questions to ask yourself could be basic ones about your own performance, such as:

How long did you talk for and did you allow enough time for the learners to feedback?

How good was the interaction with the audience?

Did you speak to all the learners equally or did you have particular favourites?

Did one or two of the learners try to grab the spotlight?

chapter 5 **inclusive learning**

Other help can be peer-group observation. You could ask a colleague to honestly assess your lesson and give you feedback.

You could also ask your learners to give their thoughts. A standard way to close a training session is to ask learners to complete a feedback form.

The information you gather can be helpful in many ways, so have a good hard look at it. You may notice patterns occurring in your teaching that you were not aware of. You should reflect on these and be ready to change. Teaching successfully is all about dealing with change.

It is good to discuss your feelings about your observed sessions with a supportive colleague. You may come up with some ideas as a result. You can form a discussion group that meets on a regular basis. Other useful tools are Internet research and discussion groups reported in professional journals.

Reflection is a circular process of course. As soon as you have changed something then you will want to reflect on these changes and start the process again. This is what professional development is all about.

activity

After you have run a teaching session, think and write about your own performance. Things that you may want to consider are: what you were particularly pleased with; what you would change or do differently; factors that you felt played a part in this – don't forget communication; what you will do as a consequence. Attach this to your RPJ.

RPJ

Preparing to Teach

Christina is in her probationary year and is being observed by her head of department. Christina's session is the second lesson in the basic ceramics course at NVQ level 3 in the art and design department of a further education college. The learners are between 16 and 18 years old. The session covers the preparation of a clay pot ready for firing in the kiln. Her lesson plan is brief:

- An introduction to what the learners will be learning and a further reinforcement of health and safety in the art room. She will spend time here talking about discipline in the department.

- A demonstration: she will gather the learners around her and she will demonstrate the correct way to assemble the ingredients and to make the pot. It will be turned out and the learners will each feel the consistency of the clay prior to working with it and afterwards.

- A practical session in which the learners prepare the pots themselves, clear away and leave the pots for the assistant to put into the kiln.

All went well until near the end of the session when some learners finished before the others, and were clearly bored. They started flicking clay at each other, one learner hurled his finished pot at another learner and Chirstina had to intercede. She lost her temper and sent the class away before the end of the session. After the session she met with the observer and wanted to discuss the session with him. He said that Christina should start by telling him what she thought went well and what she thought she would change in future. Christina commented that she thought it was the job of her manager to tell her what she should be doing and how to solve any problems that occur.

Do you agree with Christina? What went well? What went wrong? Why do you think this happened? What things do you think that Christina left out of her lesson plan?

summary

In this chapter we learnt about the tactics for starting with a group and a session, how we set the ground rules with a group and decide on acceptable behaviour. We looked at the theories of motivation and how to apply this theory to teaching and learning in a classroom or in a workshop. How we can get the best out of the audience in front of us. All sessions need an introduction where the session plan is presented to the group; the main part of the lesson where a variety of methods are used to deliver the knowledge and skills, using variety and catering for all learning styles; and an end where information is summed up and learner reaction is judged. We looked at communication theory and how this can be applied. We saw it as a two-way process. We also considered reflection and suggested ways in which it can be helpful to teaching and training. We considered ways in which we continually develop teaching and continually learn from what we are doing. We found out how important realistic feedback can be and some methods for delivering successful feedback. The skills theme of the chapter was communication.

Resources

Herzberg, F. (1959) *The Motivation to Work* Hoboken, NJ: John Wiley & Sons Inc.

Maslow, A.H., A theory of human motivation. *Psychological Review* 50, 370–396 (1943).

In this chapter, I have learnt about:

- ☐ Establishing ground rules
- ☐ Ice-breakers and lesson starters
- ☐ Learning styles and group work
- ☐ Initial assessment of learners
- ☐ Course information
- ☐ Motivation theory
- ☐ Motivation in learning
- ☐ Motivation in teaching
- ☐ Communication in teaching
- ☐ Value of reflection in teaching
- ☐ Some techniques to use for reflecting and analysing teaching
- ☐ Feedback

assessment

subject

In this chapter you will learn the importance of assessment, the different assessment methods we can use, the importance of accurate record keeping and the ways we can feedback the results to learners.

learning outcomes

In this chapter you will learn how to:

◗ Identify different assessment methods.

Assessment criteria 5.1

◗ Explain the use of assessment methods in different contexts, including reference to initial assessment.

Assessment criteria 5.2

◗ Explain the need for record keeping in relation to assessment.

Assessment criteria 5.3

study skills
note
taking
theme

Identify different assessment methods. Assessment criteria 5.1

Study skills

Most of us take notes all the time. It is a natural method of aiding recall, planning, an essential part of the creative process and an aid to listening actively. We all take notes in a different way and the important thing to realise is that notes are personal and meant only for you.

Mind mapping, discussed in Chapter 1, is a system that can help good note-taking. Notes on their own are not an end in themselves, they are simply a way of helping you remember, helping you to plan and are good for summarising. They are essential to those of us whose style of learning is visual or kinaesthetic. Reading out and repeating notes can also help those of us who are auditory learners.

How do we judge how our learning is progressing? How do we know if learners have grasped concepts and skills? How can we tell what learning styles suit all those individuals we have in our groups? How do we know that the learners are taking the right course?

chapter 6 **assessment**

By using assessment before the course starts, at the beginning of the course, within the course and at the end we can help ourselves find out the answers to all those questions. We can judge the outcomes of individual learners and we can gauge the performance of groups. Sometimes final tests are run by outside organisations such as Edexcel, sometimes the checks are organised by the teacher, sometimes outcomes are judged by the learners themselves. Final assessment may be a combination of all three.

Reflection
Write down all the types of assessment you have experienced and your reaction to them. Do you feel differently about particular types of assessment?

activity

Why do we assess? Write down all the reasons you can think of. Discuss your findings with at least one other person.

Evidence

Assessment can:

- Tell us what knowledge and skills a learner wants or needs to acquire

- Tell us how a learner could achieve the outcomes they are aiming for

- Tell us how learners are progressing on our course or programmes

- Tell us how to motivate a learner to continue with a course

- Tell us about particular strengths and issues a learner may have

- Help you to redesign a course as learners' needs change

- Help you to redesign a course after it has been delivered and when you are reflecting on the course

- Form part of a learner's profile

- Demonstrate to the learners that a skill has been mastered

- Justify awarding a qualification.

Assessment that takes place before a course is known as initial or diagnostic assessment. It tries to find out what people already know and their particular abilities. Within a college this can be administered by another department and the results handed to the course tutor prior to interviews.

Preparing to Teach

For learners on a programme, there are two main types of assessment used by teachers.

These are known as formative and summative.

Formative assessment is used to tell us and our learners how well they are doing in an ongoing process. It is designed to form the basis of feedback. Formative assessment may tell you what you already know, but it is objective (not just your opinion) and fair. It provides reinforcement and encouragement.

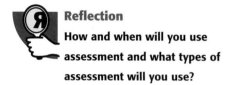

Reflection

How and when will you use assessment and what types of assessment will you use?

Summative assessment is the type that comes at the end of a course, the traditional type of tests and examinations. It is designed to find out what learners have achieved and may be administered independently by external authorities. It leads to final certificates and diplomas. Much of education and training today is driven by assessment.

case study

John has been teaching computer skills to a group of beginners at his local library as part of the government initiative to make the population computer literate. He has designed the final programme, which leads to a national award in computer literacy.

> 'I always allow each learner to develop at their own pace. When I am satisfied they have the know-how and the ability to take the test, I use a mock – an old test – to allow me to double check their performance. Entry for the exam is costly and so failure is expensive. Putting all the group in for a test at a common time can lead to failures. It doesn't do much for the learners' self-belief. They often come to me very unsure about whether they can complete this course, which they believe is essential to their future job prospects.'

What types of assessment are used by John? When and why does he use them? How typical is this process in your experience of teaching or training? Make notes about your thoughts and feelings and discuss them with at least one other person.

chapter 6 **assessment**

Explain the use of assessment methods in different contexts, including reference to initial assessment.

Assessment criteria 5.2

How and when will you assess your learners? Much depends on what you are doing with them. If the programme is for a national examination, then you are restricted by the summative assessment. The time and the place are given and you have no choice but to work towards them. However, it may be left to the individual to decided where and when assessment that informs about learners' progress is carried out. Sometimes institutions such as schools and universities set times for examinations, which have to be adhered to – even when they are internal examinations that inform us about student progress. Or you may have the flexibility to set tests or examinations when you want to, and that they can also be arranged to suit individual students.

Formative assessment gives you flexibility. Your assessments can focus on the individual needs of your learners. Assessment can be informal and may consist of you observing individual learner showing their ability to perform a particular task.

The following are types of assessment that you can use. How you use them is, in part, determined by the nature of the course or programme. Assessments can be formative or summative.

- **Initial assessment** could include learning styles and could be used to judge levels of literacy, numeracy and IT skills to discover if the learner's skills are appropriate for a particular course or training programme.

- **Formal examinations**, which can be open-book and seen papers.

- **Essays** often test the learner's ability to construct a logical argument and not necessarily their knowledge of a subject.

- **Objective tests** where the answer is already decided before the learners take the test.

- **Projects and reports** may pose problems of the ownership of the work or plagiarism.

- **Observation** is a common skills-based check that is used for NVQ-type programmes.

- **Portfolios** that give the students ownership of what they produce and can help the student to transfer knowledge.

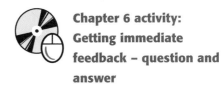

Chapter 6 activity: Getting immediate feedback – question and answer

Reflection

As explained earlier, different types of assessment are more suitable for different types of courses and programmes. What types of assessment do you feel are the best for your area of training or teaching? How would these types of assessment inform us about our leaners' progress and when is the best time to use them?

Evidence

▪ **Diaries and logs of work** that are a personal record of the learner's work, which may help them to support other forms of assessment.

▪ **Creative art objects** are used widely in creative courses where the outcome is a piece of completed art.

▪ **Questioning, interviews, orals and role-play** are frequently used to help judge how students are progressing.

▪ **Problem-solving tasks** are most often used to inform progress during the course but they can also be used at the end of a course.

▪ **Computer-based assessments** which may be supervised over the Internet.

Preparing to Teach

case study

Harriet is taking a programme which leads to a level 1 hairdressing qualification. The unit she has just taken concerns shampoo and selecting the correct type of shampoo for a client.

How would you suggest that she is assessed after the session? How will this method of assessment help Harriet?

Explain the need for record keeping in relation to assessment.

Assessment criteria 5.3

Accurate records provide useful evidence for teachers when justifying the performance of learners. Examining and awarding bodies can only validate awards when their external and internal verifiers are satisfied with courses, and the standard of the assessed work. Records helps us form pictures of learners and summative assessment helps us to establish the success of our courses and the success of qualifications nationally.

activity

Gather samples of record and mark sheets from a variety of teachers or trainers on different courses. What is the common element? How useful is each? What is the best way for you to keep records? For an individual course, discover how information about learners is recorded. Investigate the requirements of at least one examining or awarding body for one of their courses. Prepare notes or a mind map about the strengths of this particular example and discuss them with a colleague.

Reflection

What is the most suitable system for you to keep records of your learners? Produce a sample record sheet for a group you would like to teach or one you are teaching already.

Preparing to Teach

case study

Paul teaches music and is in charge of the foundation degree at a higher education college. He has a refreshing view regarding record keeping and paperwork in general. Paul says:

'I enjoy marking, assessing and paperwork. It is informative and lets me know how people are doing on their courses. It helps me to decide how they are progressing and it helps highlight the areas that students need extra help with. On a music course, the areas that the learners need support with are so many and so various it is impossible to generalise. Assessments, even on a weekly basis, are so helpful. It also gives me evidence to show the students. I find it assists when dealing with the college authorities who are concerned about the progress of the course. At the end, I find marking and recording the students' grades both satisfying and refreshing. It makes me feel I have done a good job.'

Summary

In this chapter we looked at assessment. We discovered how important accurate and consistent records are for both teachers and learners. We found out that records are also required by the organisations that employ us by and by the various authorities that approve and run the courses we teach.

In this chapter, I have learnt about:

- [ ] Assessment
- [ ] Record keeping
- [ ] Organisation requirements
- [ ] The requirements of examining and awarding bodies

Preparing to Teach

congratulations!

You have reached the end of Preparing to Teach, which will give you threshold status to teach in the Lifelong Learning Sector. Your tutor will talk to you about the assessment requirements to complete Preparing to Teach in the Lifelong Learning Sector (PTLS), and about what you need to do to progress further. Part of this will be to complete the reflective practice journal (RPJ) and to submit all assessed work.

You are now in a good position to judge if teaching, training or tutoring is really the career for you. You should now be aware of the commitment involved and how suitable a career it is for you. In this course we have covered many aspects of teaching (see opposite).

This is just the introductory phase (level 3). The next two phases will carry on from this and further develop your training. The final qualification will be a licence to practise as a Qualified Teacher in the post-16 sector (QTLS).

Learning checklist

- The origins of teaching
- Your early experiences of teaching
- The RPJ
- Mind maps
- The qualities of a teacher
- Learners and their expectations
- Teaching as a job
- Job description
- Responsibilities and roles
- Identify learner needs
- Keeping up to date and informed
- Ensuring equality
- Ensuring inclusion
- Ensuring Health and Safety considerations are included in all sessions
- Unusual skills in your area
- Unusual learning styles
- An introduction to Bloom
- Knowledge, skills and attitude

- A CV for teaching
- Observing a teacher or trainer
- A checklist to use
- Learning skills
- Skills in our area
- Embedding common skills
- Planning theory
- Planning practice
- Time management theory
- Time management practice
- Schemes of work and training proposals
- Session plans
- The learning cycle (after Kolb)
- Importance of variety
- Importance of humour
- Importance of understanding individual learners
- Resources
- Establish ground rules

- Ice-breakers and the start of lessons
- Learning styles and group work
- Initial assessment of learners
- Course information
- Motivation theory
- Motivation in teaching
- Communication theory
- Communication in teaching or training
- The value of reflection in teaching or training
- Some techniques to use for reflecting and analysing teaching
- Assessment
- Record keeping
- Organisation requirements
- Feedback

glossary and index

Glossary

CURRICULUM VITAE – the Latin name for a description of what you have achieved to date. Usually abbreviated to CV.

DIFFERENTIATED LEARNING – learners are all different. A differentiated session involves learners in being active decision makers and problem solvers. Differentiated learning is more natural and effective than sessions where learners are treated as passive receivers of information.

DfES – stands for the Department for Education and Skills, a government department (www.dfes.gov.uk).

EDEXCEL – an awarding body. The name is amalgamated from education and excellence (www.edexcel.org.uk).

EV – external verifier. An individual who represents an awarding body. EVs check the work of learners and teachers to maintain standards of quality.

EXPERIENTIAL – learning by doing or through experience

FUNCTIONAL SKILLS – an umbrella title for a range of skills, such as literacy, numeracy and ICT.

GCSE – the general certificate of secondary education

ICE-BREAKERS – exercises to get learners involved and focused at the start of a session or a group of sessions.

ICT – Information communication technology. The use of computers in a wide sense to aid and support learning.

IV – internal verifier. An individual who checks the work of learners and teachers to maintain standards of quality within an organisation.

INTERACTIVE – a programme that responds to user activity.

LLLU – London Language and Literacy Unit.

LLUK – Lifelong Learning UK is responsible for the professional development of all those working in libraries, archives and information services, work-based learning, higher education, further education and community learning and development (www.lifelonglearninguk.org).

MOVE ON – a website that offers support and advice about skills for life (www.move-on.org.uk).

NVQ – National Vocational Qualifications, a range of work-based qualifications.

OFSTED – Office for Standards in Education (England) (www.ofsted.gov.uk).

QCA – a non-departmental public body, sponsored by the DfES. QCA regulate and develop the curriculum, assessments, examinations and qualifications (www.qca.org.uk).

RPJ – reflective practice journal: a document you complete on this course to encourage you to think about your teaching.

RESOURCES – things that can be used to support or help a session.

SVUK – The Standards Verification UK is a subdivision of LLUK that is currently working on the verification of initial teacher training.

VAK – learning styles: visual, auditory and kinaesthetic.

Index (g indicates a glossary term)